Productivity & Accelerated Learning
2 In 1 Bundle

Master The Secrets Of The Successful Through Unlimited Memory Improvement, Time Management, Goal Setting & NLP Self Discipline To Cure Procrastination And Laziness

Adam Hunter

NLP Productivity

Reach Success Using Neuro-Linguistic Programming Transformational Confidence Creator Life Habits 2.0: Goal Setting, Time Management, Morning Routine, Leadership and Increase Energy

Adam Hunter

Table of Contents

- NLP Productivity 2
- Introduction 8
  - Importance of Habits 10
  - Mistakes 12
- What Do You Want? 14
- NLP 20
  - Creating Reality 20
  - Adding Structure 21
  - Benefits of NLP 21
  - Needed Attributes 22
  - NLP History 22
  - How NLP Works 24
  - It Can Change Your Life 25
- Increase Energy 26
  - Main Elements 32
  - Five Questions to Find Your Purpose 37
  - Food 37
  - Sleep 40
  - Exercise 41
- Self-Discipline 44
  - Reward Yourself 46
  - Habits 48
  - Hacks 51
  - Mistakes 54
- Goal Setting 57
  - Breaking Down Goals 61
  - Mistakes 62
- Time Management 64
  - Productivity Hack 67
  - Mistakes 71
- Morning Routine (Make This a Habit for True Success) 73
  - Steps for Success 77

The Truth about Productivity and Self-Esteem That No One Has Told You 82
30-Day Challenge 88
Conclusion 94
Accelerated Learning 97
Introduction 101
Covering the Basics (Insane Focus) 106
    Kill Multi-Tasking 106
    Focus on One Thing 107
    Be Present 108
    Imagination 110

Unlimited Memory 112
    Use Your Imagination 112
    Create Pictures 114
    The Rule to Remember Anything 117

Photographic Memory 122
    Pages, Words, and Lists 122
    Numbers 128
    Places 132
    Names 134
    Mind Mapping 137
    Increase Reading Speed 141

Maintaining Memory 149
    Review 149
    Naps 151
    Meditation 153

Turning Procrastination into Productivity 155
    Purpose 158
    Goals 162
    Time Limits 165

Interesting Facts 168
    Foods 168
    Coffee and Gum 168

Bad Habits that Slow Memory and Decrease Productivity 173
    Smoking and Drinking 173
    Exercise 174
    Sleep 176

Conclusion **179**

© Copyright 2019 - All rights reserved.

The following eBook is reproduced below with the goal of providing information that is as accurate and reliable as possible. Regardless, purchasing this eBook can be seen as consent to the fact that both the publisher and the author of this book are in no way experts on the topics discussed within and that any recommendations or suggestions that are made herein are for entertainment purposes only. Professionals should be consulted as needed prior to undertaking any of the action endorsed herein.

This declaration is deemed fair and valid by both the American Bar Association and the Committee of Publishers Association and is legally binding throughout the United States.

Furthermore, the transmission, duplication, or reproduction of any of the following work including specific information will be considered an illegal act irrespective of if it is done electronically or in print. This extends to creating a secondary or tertiary copy of the work or a recorded copy and is only allowed with the express written consent from the Publisher. All additional right reserved.

The information in the following pages is broadly considered a truthful and accurate account of facts and as such, any inattention, use, or misuse of the information in question by the reader will render any resulting actions solely under their purview. There are no scenarios in which the publisher or the original author of this work can be in any fashion deemed liable for any hardship or damages that may befall them after undertaking information described herein.

Additionally, the information in the following pages is intended only for informational purposes and should thus be thought of as universal. As befitting its nature, it is presented without assurance regarding its prolonged validity or interim quality. Trademarks that are mentioned are done without written consent and can in no way be considered an endorsement from the trademark holder.

Introduction

Do you know what it means to have a productive mindset? A productive mindset means that you use your resources the best that you can. Your resources are your efforts, energy, and time. It means that you aren't trying to do everything or trying to do things the quickest way possible. It is making the best and most of the things you have while enjoying yourself. In order to do this, there are a few characteristics or qualities that can help you in accomplishing this.

These include:

- Curiosity – You are willing to explore, question, and seek out new concepts and ideas. You want to learn and understand more than you already do.

- Motivation or Desire – Without these things, you don't have anything to drive you to improve and progress. Inertia is what happens when you don't have the desire and it destroys progress.

- Vision – You are able to see what you want and this will give you focus and ideas of what you would like the outcome to be. Without this in mind, it would be hard to strive for your goal.

- Critical Thinking – Having the ability to assess different situations objectively or to see things how they really are. You are able to look at the pros and cons and you can make appropriate adjustments.

- Self-Confidence – Having the belief and faith that you are completely able and can do whatever you want. Without this, you won't be able to reach your full potential.

- Persistence – The majority of things won't come easily. You have to be willing to overcome adversity. You have to challenge yourself and persist so that you can reach your goals. Never let your circumstances, other's opinions, or setbacks keep you from reaching your goals.

- Positive Outlook – Your attitude, no matter negative or positive, will make or break you. Having a positive attitude will allow you to reach anything, but a negative mindset will defeat you before you get going.

- Open-Minded – An open mind allows you to create innovative new ideas. You will be open and receptive to new experiences.

- Balance – In order to function well, it's important that you remain balanced. It's important to work towards goals, but you have to take time to recharge and rejuvenate. Pushing yourself too much or trying to do too much will end up causing you to become frustrated and burned out.

By making sure that you follow the elements above in your life, you will create a productive mindset and set yourself up to reach your goals in a more effective manner, develop good habits, and improve your mind to function better. You have more time than you believe you have. You aren't busy. Actions will bring the results that you are looking for and your future self will thank you for it. NLP has the ability to help you with this.

It's amazing to find out how quickly you can learn how to switch up your habits when you want to. Eating, nail biting, smoking, and sleep habit can be changed using NLP. People who use NLP to change their lives are often skeptical about how quickly it can happen. Things can change in one session. In one case, a man was able to use a small NLP technique that took 25 seconds to break a 17-year-old nail biting habit.

People have been able to give up lifelong habits in a single session. NLP can give you the mental tools that you need to be successful in your life. One of the main things about NLP techniques is that you will step out of yourself and view yourself in the light that you want to as an observer.

This probably sounds very simple, and you could be saying "What's the big deal?" But when you actually do these things in a specific way, in a very deliberate way, you will be able to make a mental image so compelling that you attract it into your life. You will become a magnet getting pulled away from your old self and into your new self as the person who is no longer held down by their old habits.

You will become the person that you have always wanted to be. The reason NLP works so well is that you will be dissociated and you will see yourself in your mind in a compelling and new way. This process has a lot of magic and power. The key to NLP techniques is repetition, visualization, and imagination.

Since the unconscious mind is unaware of what is real and what isn't, a new habit has the ability to be created through mental repetition and rehearsal. In fact, a lot of professionals will use mental rehearsal to improve their work. Mental rehearsals can help you to change your habits without having to physically repeat it over and over again. In many NLP techniques, you will associate your new behavior with a specific trigger. This trigger could be a feeling or an object such as a telephone. When you repeatedly associate that trigger with your new habit, you will start to create a habitual response that will end up being triggered when the trigger is presented.

Importance of Habits

Habits are what makes or breaks success. Even though they are important, very few people know how to make habits work. A lot of people will associate the word habit with negative things like a drug or gambling habit. But the majority of habits are positive, like meditating, exercising, or starting a project long before it is due.

A habit is something that you do regularly without having to consciously decide to do it. It's an automatic behavior. Habits are what allow you to do things without having to use a bunch of mental effort. They are what make your everyday life possible.

There are a lot of people who try hard to break bad habits. Dieting is the big one. When a person chooses to follow a diet, they are trying to break the habit of overeating or eating bad foods. A lot of alcoholics and smokers want to break their habits, and there are just as many supporters out there who are willing to help them.

Over the last several decades, researchers have come to realize how important habits are. Here's a powerful story of the importance of habits. In 1993, Eugene Pauly was rushed to the hospital with a 105-degree temperature, vomiting, and stomach cramps. He was diagnosed with viral encephalitis. He was in a coma for ten days, and when he came to, his wife had to face the fact that he was no longer Eugene. He was still able to speak, but he didn't know the day of the week, could recall conversations, would cook breakfast but not eat it, fall asleep, and then fix the same meal a little while later.

A scan discovered that the virus had almost destroyed his medial temporal lobe, which controls recall functions and emotions. Eugene and his wife moved so that they were close to their daughter and one of the main and most important parts of his daily habits was walking around their block. Doctors had told his wife that Eugene needed to be under constant supervision. If he were to get lost, he wouldn't be able to make it back home. I mean, he couldn't even tell you what door in his house led to the kitchen.

His wife got up one morning and got dressed. When she went to find Eugene, he wasn't there. She ran out into the neighborhood screaming for him because even a person tried to help him, he wouldn't be able to tell them where he lived. The doctors have told her, in no uncertain terms, that he would never be able to find his way home. She went home not knowing what to do. Guess what she found?

Eugene was watching the history channel and a pile of pinecones laid on the table that he had collected on his walk. Repetition is what allowed him to do this. When you do something often enough, what is known as chunking will take place. The brain will change a series of conscious actions into something automatic that doesn't have to be thought about. Eugene formed a habit.

Mistakes

Starting a journey towards productivity is an amazing thing. The problem is that a lot of people will make mistakes that can be avoided. Let's look at the top five.

1. Not having a clear vision

People who are focused on being productive will start trying to do things better and faster and will end up forgetting the main point of what they are doing. Focusing too much on the 'how' will cause you to forget the 'why'. If what you are doing isn't meaningful, then why is it so important that you can do so much of it?

2. Multitasking

Everyone wants to get as much done as they can and multitasking may seem like a good idea but it won't help you. The human brain does better when you focus on a single task at a time. If you are reading something while talking to somebody else, you aren't going to retain much of the information. Multitasking ends up being counterproductive.

3. Using too many tools and systems

There are a lot of "productivity systems" out there and they can be tempting to buy all of them. Each one of them has a learning curve, so it's going to take time to learn every single one of them. This is counterproductive. Pick one system you like, learn it, and use it.

4. Taking on too much

Sure you want to get more done, but just because you are doing more things doesn't mean you are being productive. You won't be able to get everything done in the timeframe that you need to. This can also lead to burnout, which will slow you down even more.

5. *Not enough sleep*

When you try to be too productive by taking on harder and more projects, you have less time for yourself. This will cause your sleep to suffer. Nobody can function on only four hours of sleep. This is one of the biggest mistakes that anybody can make. Sleep is so important for a healthy mind and body and should never be sacrificed in the name of productivity.

With this in mind, let's look at how you can become productive in a good way.

What Do You Want?

A lot of people suffer from being too rational. They have big dreams they would like to achieve but they hold back by being too caught up in all the risks. They don't want to disrupt anything, and therefore, always play it safe.

In order to get themselves out of their comfort zone, they set goals. The process of making goals is like setting checkpoints along the road to a wanted outcome. Making and reaching little goals could serve as a way to check your progress. You can measure how far you have advanced and will show you how viable your plan is.

You need to approach setting goals just like you would a road trip. You need to create a roadmap and chart your success along the way. When you plan a long road trip, you know your destination, but because the trip is long, you need to make some stops along the way.

Before starting out, you decide you want to stop after a few hundred miles to get some food, then you will need to stop about halfway to refuel the car. Around the three-quarter mark, you decide to stop and stretch your legs and in another 100 miles, you need to stop to get more gas.

At every stop, you are meeting a small goal that will eventually get you to your final goal.

What can you do if you don't know what you want to do with your life? Not to worry, this is a problem for many people.

For some people, this isn't a problem at all. For others, it might take them a lifetime to figure it out.

It is easy to do the same thing day in and day out. It is familiar and comfortable. For people who want fulfillment in their lives, the following questions will help you see a clear picture of what you would like to do with your life:

1. *What have I already accomplished in my life?*

Think about all of your experiences and what you are the proudest of. Did these accomplishments make you feel good? Bad? Most of them probably made you feel good about yourself, right? Why not try to copy those feelings and experiences?

If you have ever signed up and finished a marathon, you probably felt very well about yourself afterward, didn't you? Why not begin training for another one? If you had children who grew up to be a musician because you taught them they could be whatever they wanted to be when they grew up, then you could be a mentor to other children.

Keep doing what makes you feel fulfilled.

2. *If there were no limits on your life, what would you choose to do or have?*

Try this: If you didn't have any limits, what would you do?

If time or money was no object, who would you spend time with? What would you love to do? Where in the world would you go?

Answering these questions could help you find out what you would like to do in life. This isn't saying you need millions to find happiness.

What it is saying is when you answer these questions, it will help you set goals, to reach milestones, and make a path to fulfillment and happiness.

Don't think about limitations and things that might be impossible, think about how much you want these things in life.

Remember, it is possible to start over and do things you really want to do.

3. *What are you most passionate about?*

When you want to have a very fulfilling life, you have to think about things that you are passionate about.

You absolutely have to know what you are passionate about so you can figure out what makes you happy and drives you. Ask yourself this:

What "jobs" have you done that don't feel like "jobs"? What makes you feel fulfilled? What things do you love? Do you like writing? Do you love being around animals? Do you like taking pictures of things?

The main point is, find out what you absolutely love to do and do more of it.

4. *Are there any people in the world you admire?*

If you follow the same path that successful people walked, you could have the same success.

Think about all the people you admire and respect. What qualities do they possess? Could you learn anything from them? What about them makes you respect them?

You are the average of the five people that you spend the most time with. Never waste time with people who tell you that you can't reach your dreams.

Spend as much time as possible with optimistic, successful, happy people and you might turn out just like them.

5. *Do you have any goals in your life?*

Goals are necessary if you want a happy future. Answer these questions:

- What goals do you have for your family?
- What goals do you have for your career?
- What goals do you have for your health?

When you have answered these, you will have a better idea of what you need to do in life.

6. *Are there things you don't like doing?*

One way to figure out what you would like to do with your life is to honestly assess the things you don't like to do.

What things do you absolutely despise? Are there things about your current job that you don't like?

You might not like meetings but you have to sit through hours of them each day. If this is happening, find a career where you could work alone more.

The main idea is if you want to change your life, you have to take action. This brings us to the last point.

7. *Are you willing to work hard to get what you want?*

Amazing accomplishments don't come easy. You will need to make a huge effort if you want great things out of life. This means you will have to put in more hours than normal people. Get outside your comfort zone and learn everything you can so you can achieve everything you want to achieve.

Here's the best part: most of the time the journey is more fulfilling than the actual goal. It is during these insignificant, little moments that you will find an "aha" moment that will help you answer this question:

"What exactly would you like to do with your life?"

To help you answer this question, you need to make a personalized map to arrive at your goal by making the following types of goals: stretch, immediate, and intermediate.

Stretch Goals

Begin by creating a long-term goal that might take several years to reach it. Figure this out first since this goal is going to influence your immediate and intermediate goals.

Stretch goals need to be huge. Some of these goals might be more specific than others. One very specific stretch goal might be buying a million dollar home. A vague goal might be wanting to be a producer of a television show. A very vague goal would be working in the fashion industry.

It is fine to leave room for some interpretation. Be as specific as you can and leave room for adjustment. When you create a stretch goal, you can work out the checkpoints on the way.

Immediate Goals

You need to make immediate goals that are small enough that you will be able to meet them within a week. These goals should be more like activities that could be done easily in one week.

Ask yourself this question: What do I have to do this week that will help me move along toward my goal? What little things could I do that will move me closer to that goal?

If you are a writer, one goal might be to write for 30 minutes every day. You might be looking for a career change and you found a book that is about the field you want to enter. You could make an immediate goal to read that book. Make sure these immediate goals are realistic. Being able to accomplish these immediate goals should feel like baby steps. They will help you with your overall growth and development along with setting you up to finish your intermediate goals.

Intermediate Goals

These goals are broader than your immediate goals and might have monthly or even yearly goal.

One intermediate goal could be to apply for a training program or apprenticeship. If your goal requires you to relocate, quitting a job, or enrolling in school, set a deadline for making one of these steps happen.

Meeting intermediate goals will help you move forward toward your goal. Reaching them might shove you out of your comfort zone but that is fine. Discomfort helps us grow and become the person we want to be.

Now that you have answered all the questions and know how to set goals, stop and take the first steps toward making your life better. Set your goals because you are going to need them later. You will be able to look back at these each day if you truly want to be successful.

NLP

Many people ask the question: What is NLP? Well, simply NLP is Neuro-Linguistic Programming. It is an approach that offers people tools and techniques that will help them deal with life's challenges and opportunities. It is a practical discipline that wants to bring results into the world.

So, basically, NLP is studying what works and the situations that they work in.

Let's break down NLP into individual words and learn more about it.

Neuro relates to the body's nervous system. The way our nervous system functions gets influenced by information that we take in through all our senses. If we can learn to take in information accurately, we will listen better and be more observant. If we can be more open to feelings of our own and others, our brains will receive better information to help us make the best decisions for us. We will, therefore, be able to communicate both unconsciously and consciously better.

Linguistic deals with language. When we are more aware and can understand words along with their structure and how they are spoken, their rhythm, voice tone, and speed, the information we get from this will help us make decisions and communicate unconsciously and consciously.

Programming is referring to habits. Everyone develops habits, some are useful, some aren't. NLP will teach us how we will be able to develop and use helpful habits and get rid of habits that aren't useful.

Creating Reality

One belief of NLP is everyone is responsible for building their own map of reality.

These maps get filtered by our nervous system, beliefs, experiences, and senses. Basically, most of the challenges we face are based on how we perceive the world and not the world itself. This is similar to confirmation bias, cognitive dissonance, worldview, and mental maps.

If we had the ability to improve how we take in and use the information that we get from our senses, then we will be able to improve our performance.

Adding Structure

We need to be aware of, listen to, and notice how and what people feel, hear, and see. Being able to understand our senses and how they affect others and ourselves will help us develop strategies that will guide our behaviors.

NLP is guiding and leading others and ourselves. It isn't about forcing, tricking, or telling. It's about figuring out what is constructive for everyone.

Keeping all that in mind, my definition of NLP is: "NLP explores how we act, communicate, and think. It is how we imitate and improve on performance in many different activities. We then transfer the things we've learned onto other people."

Benefits of NLP

- Helps you connect to your motivation, values, and purpose.
- Your life will be more fulfilled and successful.
- Your performance at work will improve. You might even begin building and starting your own company.
- You will have better relationships at home and work.

- You will develop better, healthy routines.
- You will overcome blocks and constantly learn new skills.
- You will enjoy your hero's journey in your life.

Needed Attributes

There aren't any special skills needed to begin exploring NLP. Having an attitude of tenderness, fierceness, playfulness, and curiosity are useful but not necessary. When you want to find results while learning about NLP, being honest, open, courageous, and ambitious helps a lot.

NLP History

NLP was created by John Grinder and Richard Bandler about 40 years ago. They worked and studied under Fritz Perls, Virginia Satir, and Milton Erickson. These are all very talented therapists and psychiatrists during their time. They decided to look at a different approach. They wanted to bring measurable changes instead of just creating another theory.

Grinder and Bandler wanted to find out what strategies great performers used, how they did it, and what they did. They created ways to model these strategies so other people could replicate the performance. This became the first model of NLP.

They constantly refined and tested their subjects. When other groups heard about the benefits, NLP began to spread across many aspects of businesses, sports, arts, coaching, and any human endeavors.

Robert Dilts is an early pioneer of NLP. He is still doing great work with entrepreneurs in Silicon Valley. His concepts about logic are useful for businesses and individuals. Every level is important along with the alignment between them. There is always one level that will be a "sweet spot" for every person or business's development. Take a look at this breakdown:

- Purpose
    - What do you want?
    - What things would you like to contribute to other people?
- Identity
    - Who are you?
- Beliefs and values
    - What are your beliefs about the world?
    - What are your beliefs about yourself?
    - What is important to you?
    - Why do you act the way you do?
- Capabilities
    - What do your strategies look like?
    - How do you come up with a plan?
    - What capabilities and skill do you possess?
- Behavior
    - What actions do you take?
    - What do you do?
- Environment
    - When and where do you do what you do?

How NLP Works

Has there ever been a time in your life when you wanted to change bad behavior and do something totally different just to realize you fell right back into your old habits?

If you have ever wondered why we repeat old habits constantly, it is because limiting behaviors and negative emotions are stronger than our conscious minds. Because patterns and habits get generated and stored by our unconscious minds, we have to make a change at the unconscious level.

If we could just say: "I'm giving that up right this minute", then we wouldn't need any therapists.

Beliefs and behaviors that are unwanted were learned and stored on an unconscious level. These don't serve us any longer so we need to change them. When you were younger, you might have learned not to like peanut butter because you had a sibling that was allergic to peanut butter. There wasn't ever any peanut butter in the house so you never knew what it tasted like. You grew up thinking peanut butter was gross or bad for you. This got stored at an unconscious level and now you still don't know what peanut butter tastes like. This is an automatic response that you can't change consciously. They can only be changed at an unconscious level.

This is true with beliefs. You might let a belief that was formed when you were young continue to hold you back now. Such as, "I never finish anything I start." This is just a belief. It isn't true and can be changed on an unconscious level to something that will empower your life.

Most of the time, people don't realize how and why they do things. This is where NLP comes into play. It will help you understand and see how you can change your behaviors and responses that no longer work for you to ones that will give you a fuller, richer life. This is your life, get out there and live it.

It Can Change Your Life

NLP could help you with your fears. This isn't just referring to phobias about creatures or insects. This is talking about fears like being afraid of other people or public speaking. NLP could be used to develop confidence by ingraining the belief that you are brave enough to stand in front of a crowd. It can encourage you by telling you that you matter in society and aren't just another face in the crowd. NLP can help you overcome depression or low self-esteem.

NLP could also help you achieve your goals. With NLP, you can find your weaknesses and reprogram your brain in a way that will empower you and overcome your weaknesses. Many athletes today are turning to NLP to improve their abilities so they will be able to excel in their field. They aren't just pushing their bodies but they are pushing their mental capacities to greater heights. Just think about what you might accomplish if you just set your mind to do something and then use these techniques to help you.

NLP could also help you with your personality. It can teach you how to understand others. It could help teach you how to understand the emotions and feelings of others. You should start treating others better and motivate them to reach for their goals. Others might begin to see a change in your personality and you might begin attracting more friends or people that just want to be around you just because you are giving off positive vibes. Some people might look to you as their role model. Keeping that in mind, you might actually begin "coaching" others. They might even thank you for helping them achieve their goals.

Increase Energy

It is amazing when we realize that our moods can affect our energy. Negative and gloomy moods can blend together to become a habitual attitude.

What is more impressive and possibly scary is the way our moods affect our energy levels. What we think about and dwell upon will determine if we are going to feel lethargic and tired or vital and alert.

Yes, you can feel tired after a long day at work. Most of the time, we feel tired because we "think" we feel tired.

Could this possibly be true? Could your emotional state and outlook truly affect the amount of energy you have daily? Is this just a theory?

With NLP, it is thought that personal experiences are more convincing than research. You need to test all things, including this. This can be done in just a few minutes.

Compare these scenarios to figure out how your mood can affect your energy levels. You need to do these instead of just reading about them.

Read the description of each scenario and then just stop and think about it for a few minutes. Then get rid of it by getting up and moving around.

Continue this with each scenario.

Scenario One

Take a few minutes to relax and be able to experience this:

"It is in the middle of winter. It is Monday morning.

It is gloomy, dark, rainy, and cold. You hear the traffic going by. You know you have a heavy workload facing you when you get to work because another co-worker is on vacation and you are covering for them this week.

You also have to attend a very boring, two-hour meeting as soon as you get to work. You check your mail and find your credit card bill. It's a lot higher than you thought it was going to be."

At this very moment, how do you feel?

How much energy do you feel you have right now? If this was happening to you, would you:

- Be ready to meet and take on your work challenges?
- Look at the world with a smile on your face?
- Be walking with a spring in your step?
- Be running up and down the step?
- Be bouncing around?

Probably not. Many people will feel drained, deflated, and low thinking about all this.

Now get up and move around. Get ready for the next one...

Scenario Two

This scenario is a bit different. It is the same day with everything exactly the same except for one thing...

"It is in the middle of winter. It is Monday morning.

It is gloomy, dark, rainy, and cold. You hear the traffic going by. You know you have a heavy workload facing you when you get to work because another co-worker is on vacation and you are covering for them this week.

You also have to attend a very boring, two-hour meeting as soon as you get to work. Right before you leave for work, you get some wonderful news...

- Someone that you have liked for a long time sends you a text and wants to meet sometime this week.
    - How will this affect your work?
    - How much energy do you have right now?
    - Do you feel light as a feather or heavy?
- You received a large amount of money. It isn't large enough that you are able to give up your job, but you will be able to do a lot with it…
    - What emotions are going through your mind right now?
    - Is this going to change your energy levels for work?
    - Did this make you smile?
- You just received a phone call saying that interview you went on last week and now your dream job is within reach. You get to begin this new chapter in four weeks…
    - Does this make you want to go to work?
    - Are you running around jumping for joy?
    - What is your energy level?
- Your partner has just called you from her doctor's appointment and told you that she is pregnant. You've been trying for a long time…
    - Will this affect your work performance?
    - What emotions are you feeling?
    - What kind of mood are you in?

How different is your mood from the bad news to the good news?

Have a Stimulating Day

Never have a nice day, have a stimulating day. The way we think and what we think about will affect your energy. Constantly being negative and gloomy will erode your optimism if you don't pay attention to the way you live each day.

Wait, there's more...

Being optimistic and cheerful is not easy if you only try to do it mentally. It isn't all about the mind. You have to manage the way you live your life daily so your activities and routines stimulate you physically and mentally.

The good news is this doesn't mean you have to wake up earlier and work out until you are totally exhausted before you even go to work.

Body Affects Mind

Most people feel completely exhausted from time to time. At times they may have a reason to feel that way like when you have been working hard, experiencing stress, or working out a lot.

Sometimes it is just living through an ordinary daily life with all its struggles and routines that cause physical and mental weariness.

We get into ruts and start focusing on what isn't going right in our lives or the bad things that could happen. This will affect the way we move, sit, and stand. We begin slumping over. We walk slower. Our faces aren't animated. Gravity feels as if it is pulling us down.

These physical and mental patterns become normal. Our attitude will change and we begin to think "this is the way I am now" and just place to blame on our genes or age. This bleak attitude will even come up with more evidence that supports it.

What Can We Do?

Many people say the only way to fix this is by changing your diet. True, at times, being tired could be due to a lack of vitamin C and B, potassium, or magnesium. I haven't found anybody who has gotten rid of this type of tiredness by taking supplements. You would be better off by eating a healthy diet and eating meals at regular intervals.

Other people will tell you that you need to exercise. This is another good idea but when you are already feeling exhausted, thinking about exercise just makes you feel more tired. The answer might be undemanding and simple: you need to get out of your rut a little bit at a time.

Change Routines

Think about the last time you took a vacation. It doesn't have to be a long vacation either. Just taking a few days to get away from it all, seeing different locations, people, food, finding fun things while away, not worrying about things will give you a boost of energy. Before you realize it, you are looking at life differently.

You will be looking at yourself and others differently.

This is the main reason why people get tempted to move their holiday destinations. It never works because we love routines and those routines will bring us back to our same old attitudes.

Being stuck in routines will quench your joy to live. Even changing up your routine a little bit could break the cycle of boredom.

Ten Percent New

Everyone deserves a routine that will make their lives run effectively so they can get things done more efficiently.

Those routines that never end and never change are not useful. You need to balance this out by offering yourself the ten percent new. This will challenge you to do something new each day for two weeks.

Some simple things you could do:

- Talk to new people
- Try new foods
- Dress differently
- Pick a new location to shop in
- Go out to eat in the middle of the week
- Change up the order you do things
- Drive to work using a different route

This list is potentially endless as you can add your own.

Basically, you just want to begin making small changes and stick with it for two whole weeks. Stand back and feel the difference.

You could keep a journal to keep track of what you do and what happens but this would be for people who are skeptical or like keeping journals. If you already keep a journal, by all means, keep track of this but if you don't, then you don't need to start just to keep track of what you are doing.

Just Ten Percent?

For many people, changing a lot of things won't work well. It will only create resistance. It won't be efficient and will only disrupt. It is hard to keep up the momentum.

You have to stick with little changes. This is why the ten percent difference is better than 90 percent. This introduces us to make small adjustments and this is enough to get you out of daily ruts. If you make a ten percent change each day or so, think about the difference this can make in a year's time.

Why are Focus, Energy, and Time Important?

Your focus, energy, and time aren't limitless. Each of them is going to run out at some time. We need to use them wisely to get the most out of these resources. This is why being organized and planning pay off.

Before You Start

If you don't begin a plan by being clear in these four areas, it will be completely wasted.

- Direction: Where do you see yourself in years to come?
- Make simple goals along the way to check your progress.
- Main focus areas that will lead to tasks you need to work on right now.
- Main areas to develop: what attributes and skills are needed to reach your end goals.

Main Elements

Being organized isn't all that hard. It does require some persistence, time, honesty, courage, and ambition. It could be a lifelong project so you need to begin soon.

The best approach for most people is to begin small. Choose something that attracts you and works on it until it has become a new habit. Now add on the next piece of the puzzle.

You have to figure out what works for you.

After some time, you will have built up some confidence and momentum. Now would be a good time to go back and begin with a new sheet of paper and figure out how you want to approach every day from scratch. Remember to use the elements you found that work for you.

1. *Make Priorities*

You can't manage your focus, energy, and time if you don't know what is important to you. This is why you need to use the discovery phase.

The next step would be to set three priorities for the next year. This would be broken down into three-month goals, monthly goals, weekly goals, and daily goals. This means that you will know what your main priorities are at the beginning of each day. You might need to change them due to events that happen in your life, but that would make it a conscious choice.

It is great to review these daily. When beginning to do this, it might seem theoretical but once you make it a habit, it will suddenly make complete sense.

2. *Improve Focus and Energy*

You can't make time so you need to find things that will improve your focus and energy. These could include when you eat, what you eat, hobbies, meditation, relaxing, rest, and exercise.

If it is important to you, include them in your daily routines. They will improve your effectiveness.

3. *Daily Routines*

Creating routines and beginning new tasks will take energy but maintaining them won't be as hard. The key is to create some routines that help to support you. Try to clarify your priorities, evening and morning questions, and mentally think about how you want your days to go. Whatever focus, relaxation, eating, and exercising routines work for you, you need to do them.

After you have established these habits, they won't take that much energy or time and gives you the freedom to use the majority of your focus, energy, and time on things that are important during that moment in time.

4. Timeboxing and Hotspots

Every hour isn't the same. There will be times during your day where you can handle hard tasks. There will be times where you can't. There are times during your day when you shouldn't be working at all. It is useful to figure out when you are most effective and make sure you use this time for things that are difficult, urgent, or important. If you have to take a meeting during a time when you aren't at your best, prepare an agenda and rehearse when you are your best.

It would be best if you could give the main tasks sufficient time. Starve less important tasks by not giving them a lot of time. What you can do within that time will be good enough.

5. Stacking Questions

Great questions will lead your emotions and thinking. These will also lead your behavior. You need to keep a list of questions to situations that you might find yourself in.

For example:

- What will you stop doing? Can you outsource or delegate?
- What will you accept? You might not want to but you have to.
- What will you maintain?
- What will you begin doing or do more of?
- Will it be worth doing this? Can you invest the energy or time to make a difference?

- Are you being productive or just being active?
- Do you have three priorities for the day?
- Do you have three priorities for the week?
- Do you have three priorities for the month?
- Do you have three priorities for the next year?
- Where are you going?
- Is there any way you can help?
- Do you have any suggestions?

6. *Begin, sometimes sprint, always finish*

You need to set beginning and finishing times. Start off fresh. If your start isn't what you thought it should be, it is fine to begin over. Sprinting can be very helpful. No matter what you need to finish and have a way to finish. Make sure you close any open loops.

7. *Designing an Environment*

It is important to have people around you that will keep you creative, energized, on track, and focused. Your work environment can have the same impact, from the pictures, the color of the walls, reminders around you, or if your space is neat could either push you forward or hold you back.

Placing affirmations around you so they catch your attention can also keep you on track.

When you can, pick the people you work with and the environment you work in.

Just Begin. It Will Be Worth It

When you begin trying to get organized, the challenge will look impossible. The demands on your attention and time are hard and you might begin to feel like you won't ever have the energy or time to begin. It is just one more project that is going to take your time.

This is why you have to begin simple. Begin by setting an intention to be productive today. Figure out three things that you want to get done.

If things change throughout the day, it will be fine if you decide to change them instead of them being drowned out by distractions.

When the day is over, review it and see how everything went. Learn from the lessons the day gave you. Let them go and you can begin fresh tomorrow.

The investment is going to be worth it.

Discovering Your Purpose

Why do you need a purpose for your life? Having a purpose will be a filter for your goals, behaviors, and actions. It will tell you when you are or aren't being productive.

Dilts' Neurological Levels

On the tip-top of this is purpose. This governs everything in life.

Underneath this is identity. This is your sense of being and exactly who you are. You can have multiple identities such as mother, sister, photographer, or writer.

Next comes beliefs and values. These are unspoken rules that govern your behaviors, actions, and decisions. These are the guides to help you make tough decisions. They also help you decide what you will and won't do in your life.

Next are capabilities. This is just a different way of saying ability or skills. This is where limitations get defined.

The last two levels are environment and behaviors. The environment is the things and events that happen around us. Behaviors are what we do.

One interesting fact about this model is it creates clear distinctions between purpose, identity, and action. If you do something that society thinks is bad (this is your behavior), won't make you a bad person (this is your identity). These are two completely separate levels. What you do daily (this is your behavior), what you have been trained to do (this is your capabilities), the roles that you play (this is your identities), and your purpose might all be a bit different.

Five Questions to Find Your Purpose

Now that we've covered all that, here are five questions you need to ask yourself in order to find your purpose:

1. If you had the choice to do whatever you want with your life without any consequence, constraints, or limitations, what would you choose?
2. Have there been any recurring themes that have shown up in your life?
3. Do you have any unique talents you can give to humanity and the world?
4. What would you be willing to risk your life to do?
5. When you die after you have accomplished all you've wanted to, what would the world remember about you?

Food

The next time you feel your energy is depleted, don't reach for another cup of coffee or a candy bar. Yes, sugar and caffeine might give you a spike in energy, but you will have a crash later that will make you feel more tired than you did before.

Try these ten foods that can boost your energy naturally and leave you feeling alert all day. They can elevate your mood and even make you more productive.

- *Eggs*

These beauties are rich in protein. In order to get the protein from eggs, you don't need to drink them as bodybuilder's do. The protein will give you a steady source of energy with lots of vitamin B. Yes, they are great for building muscle.

- *Blueberries*

These berries enhance mental agility and cognitive function. They aren't called a superfood for anything. They are full of antioxidants.

- *Whole grains*

Yes, they do contain carbs but the complex carbs release steady energy through the entire day.

- *Leafy greens*

They are iron-rich that will improve levels of concentration. You aren't going to get super strength like Popeye, but leafy greens such as spinach and kale are full of iron that will help you feel energized. Fatigue is the most common symptom of iron deficiency. Spinach is full of iron. Iron will promote the circulation of red blood cells and this will make you feel more alert and will improve your concentration.

- *Popcorn*

This yummy snack is high in carbs and fiber but if you don't smother it in butter, it is very low in calories. Popcorn is a great energy booster for children.

- *Greek yogurt*

Greek yogurt is full of protein and is a great alternative for regular yogurt. It has fewer carbs and lactose that add calories. Greek yogurt can help you feel fuller longer because its protein is slow acting.

- *Spicy herbs*

Spices can boost your metabolism and gives you a boost of energy. Peppers have a compound called capsaicin that increases the metabolism and helps with digestion. Certain types might improve cognitive function.

- *Salmon*

This fish is rich in Omega 3 fatty acids. These fatty acids can elevate moods and protects against depression. Salmon is full of these fatty acids.

- *Dark Chocolate*

This yummy food contains theobromine and caffeine. Both of these will boost your energy levels. If you eat in moderation, the sugar and caffeine will not give you an energy crash. The darker the chocolate, the less sugar and the more it will boost your energy.

- *Almonds*

These nuts are full of magnesium and vitamin E. They are a great snack for an energy boost. These nuts are the most nutrient rich. They have a lot of protein to help you keep your energy through the whole day.

Sleep

Sleeping well takes more than just going to bed at the right time. Try to follow these tips to give yourself a great chance to get quality, consistent sleep every night. If you think you are doing everything possible to try and sleep but you don't have the energy to do what you love to do, you might have other problems. Talk to your health care provider about what could be causing your sleep problems.

1. Set enough time aside for sleep. Sleep is as important to your health as exercise and diet, so be sure to set aside enough time for sleep. Plan the rest of your day around that. A good night's sleep means getting seven to eight hours every night for adults, nine to ten hours for teenagers, ten hours for elementary school children, and 11 to 12 hours for preschool children.

2. Create constant habits. Since we are creatures of habit, we are normally more successful when we follow a routine. It isn't any different with sleep. From the pre-bedtime routine to going to bed, to falling asleep, and waking each morning at the same time, you will find that being constant will make it easier to fall asleep.

3. Make a sleep environment that is comfortable. Be sure your bedroom is comfortable, quiet, and cool. The bed needs to be especially comfortable. You might need to experiment and make an investment but finding a very comfortable pillow and bed will be invaluable. You spend at least one-third of your life in bed. This makes it the main area that you don't want to skimp on comfort.

4. Before bed, turn it all off. It might be your phone, tablet, computer, or television. You need to give yourself some time to relax and unplug before going to bed. Your body needs to associate your bed with sleep. These devices will ramp up brain activity instead of slowing it down. Bright lights you get from these devices can suppress melatonin production and this makes it hard to fall asleep.

5. Use sleep technology. There are many different technologies out there that could help you sleep better. ResMed has a sleep sensor called S+ that has a bedside monitor, web app, smartphone app that will help you track and understand your sleep patterns. It will then create feedback and suggestions to help you improve your sleep.

Exercise

If you are feeling sleepy, tired, sluggish, you don't have the energy to get you through your chores. Don't try to sleep in and skip the extra cup of coffee, just head to the gym.

Exercise can help keep your body fit and boost your mood. Both of these can contribute to your well-being and health. Exercise can boost several areas of wellness because it:

- *Increases endorphin levels*

Endorphins are a natural hormone in our body that gets released when we do something that requires us to use energy. They make us move. Exercise will increase these levels. It is the release of endorphins that give joggers the feeling of euphoria that many people call "runner's high".

- *Keeps your heart healthy*

Exercise can give your cardiovascular health a boost. This allows you to have more energy throughout your day. When you can do all your daily chores, you will have energy left over and won't feel as tired when all the work gets finished. For better cardiovascular health, it is recommended that you get about 30 minutes of aerobic exercise five days every week. If you want to lower blood pressure and cholesterol, try to get about 40 minutes of moderate to vigorous intensity aerobic exercise three to four times each week.

- *Will improve sleep*

Exercise lets you sleep better. When you get enough sleep, you will feel refreshed throughout your day. One study that was done on people who had insomnia had them engage in about 150 minutes of moderate intensity exercise in one week. They realized that this amount of exercise gave the volunteers a reduction in their insomnia. It also gave them a boost in their mood, too.

- *Will sharpen your focus*

Mentally, anyone will feel ready to tackle the world and energized after exercising because endorphins will boost our energy levels. Doing 24 weeks of moderate aerobic exercise can improve cognitive function like concentration. Some researchers say that high-intensity workouts won't have the same effects. Just one session of high-intensity training can improve cognitive function with respect to short-term memory tasks and attention.

What Exercise Will Give You an Energy Boost?

Any physical activity that will get your heart rate and blood going will release endorphins and this will raise your energy level. Good exercises that target the cardiovascular system will give you stamina and strengthens the heart.

An aerobic exercise is the best in helping depression symptoms. Low-intensity exercise like yoga has many benefits for your mood. Yoga can reduce anxiety and depression. Any physical activity or routine exercise can lower depression levels.

What exercises are best? That is completely up to you and the things you like to do. If you don't like doing it, it isn't going to do you any good. It needs to be something that is enjoyable. Pick things you enjoy doing like tennis, football, or basketball. Go for a bike ride in the park. Go for a walk or jog with friends. Take time for yourself and dance to your favorite music. Try a spin class, martial arts, or kickboxing.

The key is finding something that you enjoy so you will stick with it and you will soon be reaping the benefits of a regular exercise routine.

Self-Discipline

The human language can be a funny thing at times. Knowing the way our brains hear things is really very important. Take the concept of self-discipline versus being disciplined. They mean the same thing, don't they? Do they?

Being disciplined might mean you are disciplining yourself. You discipline yourself when you go to the gym every day. You discipline yourself when you hold back and don't argue. You discipline yourself when you save money rather than spend it.

What exactly is your mind hearing? Is it hearing that you are being disciplined or is it hearing you are getting punished? If somebody else disciplines you, it is punishment, isn't it? You have done something wrong so now you are getting disciplined. Is this what your mind is hearing? If so, it isn't any wonder we have problems keeping our promises.

Self-discipline means being deeply committed and focusing on what you want versus what you are wanting right now. This sounds like a choice, right? Since the word begins with "self", it is like you have made the choice of being disciplined instead of somebody else forcing us to do it.

Is there a simple definition of self-discipline? I would say that self-discipline is the art of making sure you take constant action that is in line with whatever your highest standards are. Whatever you want to do regularly in order to reach your future goal or the process of doing these things regularly is self-discipline. Is there a way to improve self-discipline? Here are some critical steps:

- You have to know what you want to do. This may sound like common sense, but you have to know what behaviors or activities you need to do and when you need to do them.

- You have to take time to realize the best way to get better at discipline is practicing it. The good part is you can practice on anything. It doesn't matter how small or large. Practicing anything regularly will improve your discipline. If it is just adding an apple into your daily routine, then you have to make sure you do it.

- Whatever you decide to do on a regular basis, you have to start at a set time and no matter how bad or good you did, you have to continue doing it at that specified time. Create your schedule around it. You need to make it a priority. You have to hold this priority sacred. Remind yourself why you do it. If you are beginning a jogging regimen, the benefits will speak for themselves. If you want to quit smoking, then the health benefits are obvious. Just figure out a time and remind yourself why you are doing it.

- This might be the hardest, but the most valuable secret that will help you deal with discipline. This part involves keeping up with the discipline. Many have experienced when we start to do something then we get tempted to stop right after starting. Here are some ways to overcome these temptations:

    o Allow yourself to see your projected future from two basic steps. Remember, it will be easier to do the discipline tomorrow if you do it every day. It will get easier with time. Imagine the rewards of continuing and ask yourself if it will be worth it.

    o Discipline helps build character and will make you a better person. Successful people are successful because they do what they like to do and they do things they don't like to do because they know it will let them have more of what they want.

    o Begin holding your valuable and sacred word inside you. We know how frustrating it can be when somebody tells you they are going to do something then they don't. Hold yourself to higher standards.

> When you tell someone you are going to do something, be sure that you do it.

Reward Yourself

You need to reward yourself when you finish a task. Why should you do that? When you reward yourself, your brain sends out positive emotions that lead to realizing your efforts that will result in positive rewards. When you do this constantly, your brain will begin to link pleasure with accomplishing goals and moving you toward your future goals. You build upon success.

When you have finished your day, write down three accomplishments. It doesn't matter how small or big. Once you have achieved a goal, celebrate. Even small rewards will be a big motivator. It might be a coffee break, a walk in the park, or a mini vacation. When you reward yourself for all your victories both little and big, it will make a huge difference.

Psychology Behind Rewards

There are many ways you can change your habits. The best one is by giving yourself a reward.

Rewards might sound a bit self-indulgent or frivolous but it isn't. Since forming better habits might be draining, rewards play a major role. When you reward yourself, you will feel contented, cared for, and energized. This, in turn, will boost our self-esteem and this will help us keep up our good habits.

Studies have shown that people who reward themselves by buying themselves a gift or watching their favorite movie gained more self-control. This is a big secret about adulthood: When you give more to yourself, you can ask more of yourself. Self-regard is not selfish.

If you don't get any rewards, you will start to feel resentful, depleted, and burned out.

While talking with a friend about giving myself rewards when I accomplished a goal, they thought it was very strange that I rewarded myself for things I should have been doing anyway. They told me that they never give themselves rewards. This made me stop and think.

First off, it didn't matter if they gave themselves rewards or if they thought they were someone who didn't give themselves rewards. When talking about habits, it seems a bit risky.

This might seem selfless or even stoic to not give yourself rewards. When people don't get rewards, they will begin to feel deprived. Feeling deprived is a bad frame of mind to keep healthy habits. When people feel deprived, they begin to feel pressured to get themselves back into balance. If you can tell yourself that you have earned a reward, that you need and deserve it, you will feel tempted to stop your good habits.

Second, I began to think that he probably gave himself rewards, he just didn't think about them as rewards. After talking for a few minutes, he did tell me that he rewards himself because each week he purchases himself new music.

In order for something to be a reward, we have to think about it as a reward. We make it a reward when we call it a reward. Once we realize it gives up pleasure, it will become a better reward. Even something as simple as a cup of tea or a book of poems could be a reward.

When I realized that I love scented candles, a whole new world of rewards was shown to me.

Everyone needs to strive to have a large variety of healthy rewards so we can recharge our batteries in healthy ways. At times, rewards won't look like a reward. To my horror, many people think that ironing is a reward. Whatever you like, use it as a reward when you hit a goal in life.

Habits

It would be great if we could push an autopilot button and our lives would just take care of itself. We wouldn't have to worry about doing our work, eating right, exercising, or chores. They would just automatically be done. Unless technology invents robots that will do all that stuff for us, our work won't disappear overnight. If we could program our behaviors as habits, it could ease some of the struggles.

With a little bit of discipline, you can create new habits that require little to no effort to keep. Here are a few tips to help you create new habits and stick with them:

1. *Commit to 30 days*

This is all the time you need in order to get a habit to stick. If you can get through this phase, it will be easier to maintain. One month is a great time block to commit to changing because it fits easily into a calendar.

2. *Do it daily*

Consistency is critical to making habits stick. If you would like to begin exercising, go to the gym each day for 30 days. If you just go a few times each week, it will make the habit harder to create. What you do every once in a while is harder to turn into habits.

3. *Begin simple*

You can't change your life in one day. It's easy to over motivate yourself and try to do too much. If you want to begin studying for two hours each day, begin with a habit of 30 minutes and expand it every week.

4. *Keep reminders*

About two weeks into forming your habits is the forgetful stage. Put reminders up to help you remember your habit every day or you might forget for a few days. If you miss out on days, it will defeat the purpose of creating habits.

5. Be consistent

The more constant you are with your habit, the easier it will stick. If you want to exercise more, go to the gym every day at the exact same time for one month. When you add in cues like time of day and where, the circumstances remain the same and will be easier to stick with.

6. Find a friend

Find somebody who will go with you and keep you motivated when you feel like you want to quit.

7. Create a trigger

Triggers are rituals that you use just before doing your habit. If you want to get up earlier, this means waking up at exactly the same time every day. If you want to stop smoking, you might wear an elastic band around your wrist and snap it each time you feel the urge to smoke.

8. Replace any lost needs

If you are giving up something to form a habit, be sure you replace it with needs you are losing. If you watch television to relax, try listening to music, reading, or meditating to replace this need.

9. Don't be perfect

Your attempts to create or change a habit will not be successful. It might take you four tries to begin an exercise routine. Then one day, you just do it without realizing it. Try your best, but expect to have some bumps along the way.

10. Use the word "but"

If you begin to think negative thoughts, use the word "but" to interrupt your thought process. Like if you were thinking: "I am not good at this, but, if I keep practicing, I might get better."

11. Get rid of temptation

Change up your environment so you won't be tempted in your first 30 days. Get rid of all junk foods, cancel your cable, throw away all cigarettes so you don't have to struggle with your willpower later on.

12. Pick a role model

Spend time around people who have the habits you are trying to create. Studies have shown that if you are around skinny people, you are more likely to be skinny too. You basically become what you are around the most.

13. Do an experiment

Don't judge yourself until a month has gone by, just use this time as an experiment in your behavior. Experiments can't fail. They will just have different results. This gives you an alternate perspective when changing habits.

14. Swish

Think about yourself doing this bad habit. Now see yourself pushing that bad habit to the side and doing the opposite. End the sequence seeing yourself in a positive light. Watch yourself pick up a cigarette, see yourself put down that nasty cigarette and snapping the elastic band around your wrist. Last, see yourself running without any shortness of breath. Do this a couple of times until you get through the pattern before doing the bad habit.

15. Write it down

Having a piece of paper with a resolution on it isn't important. Writing that resolution down is. When you write, you make your ideas clearer and causes you to focus on your end results.

16. Know benefits

Get familiar with the benefits of making a change. Find materials that will show you all the benefits of eating healthier, exercising regularly, or quitting smoking. Watch out for any changes to your energy levels once you begin any of your new changes. Imagine what it will be like at the end of 30 days.

17. Know pain

You have to know the consequences. Find realistic information about the downside of not making new habits and this will give you more motivation.

18. Do it for you

Don't think about all the things you "should" do as habits. Move your habits toward your goals and what motivates you. Empty resolutions and weak guilt aren't enough.

Hacks

When you take a moment to look at your life as it is right now, what are some of the reasons you aren't healthy, happy, or successful?

Not counting the numerous excuses, there is probably one simple reason: no self-discipline. You just don't want to do what you have to do in order to have success. If you think about it, what is it going to take for you to be successful? It isn't a secret. Everyone knows what you need to do to live healthier. Everybody knows what they need to do to perform better at their jobs, but they won't do it. Everybody knows what foods to stay away from and what ones to eat, they still won't do it.

Knowing what you should do and doing it are two different things. If you don't have self-discipline, things won't ever get done.

Having success comes from the actions you take constantly. Having self-discipline lets you do that.

Here are five ways to build self-discipline:

1. *Think long-term*

This quote from Abraham Lincoln is a favorite of mine: "The best way to predict the future is to create it". If you ever think about where you are going to be in ten years, look at your life now. Are you taking any actions to turn your goals into reality? Are you reading any books to better yourself as a person? How many new things have you learned lately? Who are you associating with? Are you doing everything possible to achieve your daily goals?

People think their lives are going to change through some magical event but this isn't true. Your life will only change to what you are willing to change. If you aren't happy right now, what are you doing to change them? If you aren't, you are only daydreaming. Nothing is going to change if you don't change a little bit each day. To quote Aristotle: "We are what we repeatedly do. Excellence then is not an act, but a habit."

2. *The enemy of success*

The enemy of success is taking the path of least resistance. If you pick everything that is easy and fun over what is necessary, you won't ever reach the happiness and success you are seeking. This is because each victory requires some sort of sacrifice. If being successful was easy, everyone would be successful. Since success in all areas of life takes sacrifices and hard work, many people won't ever reach their potential.

When you decide to not do something you know you should do, you are wasting an opportunity to grow. You are also losing confidence in yourself. You begin to look at yourself as a lazy person. You think you will never be successful. And this self-image will become a prophecy.

3. *Know in advance that you won't ever give up*

In order for you to stay strong when facing adversity, make sure you have decided in advance how you are going to respond if it happens. You have to know what you are going to do when all hell breaks loose or you will just give up. When you write out your goals, no matter how hard they are, you have to commit to making them come true. Figure out who you are going to respond when faced with setbacks and failures so you can come back better and stronger.

If you can make this commitment and don't ever break it, you will be a success at everything you set your mind to. It might not happen immediately but it will eventually happen.

4. Write your goals daily

To keep yourself discipline daily, you have to keep the big picture in mind. When you remember why you do the things you do, you will take all needed actions to get it done. You don't work hard just because you want to. You have goals you want to reach and that makes the effort worth it.

To quote Nietzsche: "He who has a 'why' to live for, can bear almost any 'how'." This is so true. If you know deep down what you would like to do and have the reasons to do them, you will do what it takes.

The big problem is we get caught up in working and reaching our goals that we forget why we began this race. We forgot why we do the things we do and get caught up in the unending to-do list. This is why many people aren't excited about life. They don't have any goals to reach.

The easiest way to fix this problem is to rewrite your goals each day and see the future the way you want it to be. Each morning after you wake up, write down the goals you have in life. This will get you motivated immediately and it will excite you to begin your day. You have to be extremely clear on what you have to do in order to succeed. After you have focused on your goals and what you want out of life, you will be able to know what you have to do to make those goals happen.

5. Obstacles will happen

Nothing that is worth having will come easy in life. You will have to make sacrifices from time to time. They might be in the form of hard work, pain, effort, and time. You will have setbacks, and when you get close to succeeding, there will be another test to see if you really want it. After passing countless tests, will you finally succeed? The biggest tragedy in life is many people give up just before they finally succeed.

To grow as a person, you have to face life's challenges to succeed. It doesn't matter how long it will take or how hard it will get, remember these words of Les Brown: "It isn't over until I win."

Mistakes

Here are the most common mistakes that will ruin your self-discipline. Prevention is better than a cure and it isn't any different when you want to build your self-control.

1. Rely on willpower

The first mistake people make is they rely on willpower rather than planning for temptations. Don't rely on willpower alone, plan for any and all temptations and place roadblocks in front of them. If you are trying to diet, don't keep unhealthy foods in your house. Throw it away or give it away so you don't have to deal with the temptation.

2. False hope

The second mistake is a syndrome called false hope. This is where you have unrealistic expectations about the consequences, ease, amount, and speed of the changes you are going to make in life. People who have problems with this syndrome will try changing themselves just to fail every time since they have set an impossible goal.

It doesn't matter how self-disciplined you are, if your expectations are unrealistic, you are going to fail. It is important to know about this phenomenon and research what goals you can achieve realistically. If you go step by step instead of reaching for the moon immediately, you will save yourself a lot of anguish.

3. Underestimating stress

The third mistake is underestimating how much of an impact stress will have. Stress can affect the amount of self-control you have. If you don't take care of your mental health, your self-discipline is going to deteriorate. To keep this from happening, introduce some habits that will reduce stress in your life. Spend 30 minutes daily doing activities that relax you. Listen to music, meet with friends, read a book, cuddle with your pet, exercise, meditate, or take a walk.

4. Neglecting the sustainability of change

The fourth mistake is neglecting how sustainable your changes are. You may be tempted to introduce a lot of changes in your life and want them to stay around forever. Even self-disciplined people need to take breaks every now and then. If you don't think about how sustainable your resolutions are, you won't be able to develop good self-discipline. To stay away from this mistake, give yourself some leeway. If you would like to lose some weight, schedule some cheat days every now and then to give yourself a break.

5. Waiting for the perfect time

The fifth mistake is trying to wait for the perfect conditions. If you keep saying I'll start tomorrow, next week, next month, next year, 99 percent of the time, you will fail. There isn't any amount of self-discipline that will help you begin a diet, start a business, learn new skills, be a better wife and mother, begin saving money or find a dream job. Begin right away or realize you don't desire your goals enough.

Goal Setting

Probably one of the most important things you can do in reaching your dreams is creating your goals. You know what you want in life, but how are you going to reach it? That's where SMART goals come in.

But, before we look at how to create your goals, let's clear up any confusion between short and long-term goals. Beyond the obvious, understanding the difference between these two things can help you to navigate your path from the present to the future with shown progress. When you work towards specifics, it helps you to bring your vision to life.

Long-term goals tend to be strategic. This is the reason why they shape the direction of your life. The success of achieving these goals is a reflection of how well you have done overall. Short-term goals show how you are doing in a specific moment in life.

Short and long-term goals have the purpose of helping you to reach your overall desire in life, whatever that may be.

Short-term goals are typically goals that you can achieve in less than five years, and more likely within one to three years. They are made up of operational components that will affect your immediate future. They also help to create the action plan for reaching your long-term goals.

Long-term goals will take more than five years to achieve, and likely upwards of 10 or more. These are the big items in life that you want to reach, such as buying a million dollar house or having your company reach a worth of a million dollars. The short-term goals you decide on will help you to reach those long-term goals. Both long and short-term goals can be planned out using the following SMART method.

SMART goals stand for Specific, Measurable, Attainable, Realistic, and Time-lined.

Goal setting is very much a prerequisite to success in almost every part of your life, but 95% of people don't set goals. SMART goals coupled with NLP helps you to go past just setting a goal and to program your mind to drive you towards your goal. First, you will create your SMART goal.

Specific – You want to bring specificity into your goal so that you can find clarity by defining what exactly your core values are. If you create a goal that is too general, it will cause challenges when it comes to creating a workable plan. Saying I want to drop 30 pounds is better than I want to lose weight.

Measurable – Measurement is what can tell you how you are progressing. The way you measure your goals should align with what motivates you the most. For example, experiencing a happier mood and more energy may be a more motivating way to measure weight loss than looking at a number on the scale.

Attainable – Most likely your goal is going to be attainable. This just means that you will actually be able to achieve your goal. Everything is attainable; just make sure that with your time and resources that you will actually be able to reach that goal.

Realistic – While everything may be attainable, not everything is realistic. You can have a goal for becoming a millionaire, but if you add a timeline of one month, that's probably not that realistic. This type of goal is setting you up for disappointment.

Time-lined – This means that you have things mapped out in a time-based manner so that you have milestones and the like to help push you along.

Now is the time to pull in the NLP. This is where you will use a WISE approach to your goals.

What

If...?

State in positive

Envision

First is the "What If...?" part. Goal setting should be creative. What ifs can cause a catastrophe if there is an attachment of anxiety to the future. However, in this case, it can lead to enlightenment to what's possible as well as the possible speed bumps you might face.

What if I achieve my goal? What if I don't achieve my goal? What if I knew I would reach my goal?

These questions will provide you with "ecology," as it is referred to in the NLP world. Basically, it means you connect with the impacts and consequences to improve your alignment with your goals.

State in positive – It's important that you word your outcomes in the positive when setting goals. This means you use words that reflect what you want instead of what you don't want.

The power of wanting something is powerful. Think about when you told yourself, "I don't want to forget to grab flour at the store." You forgot to get it, didn't you? Next time, try saying "I must remember to get flour at the store." This mindfulness in wording is what stands between you are and your goals.

Envision – This is the fun part of goal setting. You get to think about what your life could be like once you reach your goals. Making sure that all your senses get used, ask yours: When I reach my goal:

- What tastes, smells, sounds, and sights surround me? How am I going to feel?

- Who will be with me? What will they say or do?

- What do I look like? What will I say or do? What am I wearing?

- Where will I be? What is it going to look like?

NLP refers to this practice as evidence. By using SMART and WISE goals, you will be able to achieve whatever you want in life. But the important thing to remember is that you actually write down your goals by hand. One study performed on goal setting found that those who wrote down their goals by hand were more likely to achieve them. They took a group of graduating college students and asked them to set goals. Some of the group didn't set any goals, others did but didn't write them down, and then a small percentage wrote down their goals. After several years, they interviewed the same students. The students who created goals but didn't write them down made twice as much as the students who didn't set goals, but the ones who wrote down their goals made ten times as much as the ones who didn't.

Most people think just having a goal in mind is enough, but it's not. The secret to reaching your goals involves writing them down in a clear and well-defined manner.

Written goals create a reminder. You can look back at the goals every day, or whenever, to remind yourself of what you want to achieve. Humans forget a lot of good ideas. They can vanish as quickly as they come. That's why writing things down is so important. You can't forget it if it's on paper.

It's also one step into bringing your vision into reality. Writing them causes you to commit to achieving them. When they are written, people don't feel the need to work towards them.

It can also help you to track your progress. We already talked about the importance of tracking your progress. You also need to track failures, that way you don't end up repeating mistakes. When you track yourself, you will find that you are more motivated to try harder.

Lastly, written goals help you to filter opportunities. As you start to achieve success in your life, you will notice more opportunities. These opportunities can be distractions that knock you off track. To fix this problem, you have to evaluate your list of written goals on a regular basis. This will help you to identify the things that will take you off track.

Breaking Down Goals

You should now have a good understanding of how to create long and short-term goals, but right now, I want to look at why it is so important that you break down your bigger goals into actionable steps.

The first thing, when setting your goals, should be to create your long-term goals. Once you have created your long-term goals that are obtainable and have a timeline, you can move onto medium-term goals.

This is your first stepping stone to achieving your long-term goals. This should be things that you can achieve in a little less time than it would take to reach your long-term goals. They also need to be specific and have a timeline.

Lastly, you will create the small-term goals. These are the actionable steps that you can take to reach your goals. These little goals are meant to make the large goal not seem so daunting. Because, if you think that you can't reach your dreams, then you won't. Then there comes a point where you have to start planning and start doing.

- Plan and prioritize your tasks to help you decide on what is the most important.

- The first step should only take 30 minutes. If it takes longer, try to break it down so that you are less likely to procrastinate.

- Every evening, reflect on tomorrow. Pick the tasks you want to work on.

- Come up with a to-do list to improve your focus, help you feel accomplished, and reduce stress.

- Write your three most important tasks down. Start with the first and work early in the day so that you have the most willpower.

- Be realistic about what you can accomplish in a given timeframe.

Doing this and accomplishing your smaller goals will keep you motivated. It will also help you to move closer to your long-term goals.

Mistakes

People tend to make mistakes when they set goals. It doesn't mean they are bad at it, mistakes just happen sometimes. There are five main mistakes that can create problems when it comes to setting and achieving goals.

1. *The goals are too big*

A common mistake people make with their goals is creating a goal that is too big. That doesn't mean you can't achieve it, but goals work best when they are doable with where you are in life right now. It's going to be very hard to start doing something that is in complete opposition to what you are currently doing. That's why you want to create actionable and concise goals so that they are easier to achieve.

2. *Setting too many goals*

Some people will get caught up in creating goals and can create too many to the point where they are overwhelmed. This will keep them from achieving any goals because they won't know where to begin. A couple of long-term goals broken down into actionable steps that you can take every day is the best way to improve your odds of reaching your goals.

3. *Focusing on outer attainment*

When you look over your goals, how do you feel? Do they make you feel excited or do you feel dread? Goals are only reached when you focus on how you want to feel once they are achieved. You can't successfully reach goals for somebody else. You have to reach them for you. You need to ask yourself why you want to achieve your goals.

4. *Thinking it relies only on willpower*

When your goals are exciting and motivating, you will start to give yourself a pep talk in order to achieve them. But the environment you have around your goals is also important, just as much so as willpower. Willpower isn't the only thing that you need to achieve your goals. There are ways to create an environment that won't require as much willpower on your part, such as shutting off electronics so that you won't be distracted.

5. *Waiting until...*

Many people will say, "I will get started working on that on..." They think there is a better time than now to start working towards their goals. The best time to start working on your goals is now.

Time Management

Have you ever had the feeling that time was just flying by, or that it was creeping along? Are there times where you feel overworked with too much to do and not the time to do it, or you are bored to tears and can hear the clock tick every second? If yes, then you probably struggle with time management.

You are among the many who wish that a day held 48 hours because 24 aren't enough. But through the power of NLP, you would find that 24 hours is just enough.

How do you manage time?

When it comes to NLP and time management, there are two main types of people: those who work "through-time" and those who work "in-time." People who work in-time don't notice the passage of time. They live in that particular moment and they don't worry about a timeline. One example of this is web surfing. You go from site to site without any thoughts about time.

Those who work through-time are extremely aware of the passage of time, so they make sure that they plan for things. For example, this type of person would choose their next free half-hour to browse through social media.

People who are a part of one or the other category could still lack some time management abilities. However, through-timers tend to streamline their activities and manage their time better by using a few helpful techniques. It is those who live their life in-time that need innovative ways to manage their time.

The first thing that people could do is to activate the attitude of self-reflection where you take some time to think about your thought process. When you do this, you will be able to change your thinking from, "I can, but…" to "I should," to "I must," to "I will."

The second thing that can be done is creating a motivational mechanism so that you will always be inspired to do the needed tasks in the hopes of getting something back.

While a lot of people think about motivating factors, more often than not, they tend to forget about them when they are distracted or tired. NLP tools have the ability to help create a better foundation for people to keep their motivation up. NLP teaches you to be single-minded and firm in your actions so that time-wasters and distractions will not interfere.

With this in mind, I want you to do something right quick. I want you to picture the two different futures that you could when you are 90-years-old; a negative one and a positive one.

The negative future is whatever the worse possible type of future could be. You don't have any money, friends, and your health sucks, you live on the street, and you get your meals in a food kitchen. This should be the future that scares you so much that you have a resounding "no" forming in your mind.

In your positive future, you have money, friends, health, happiness, comfort, and security. You look back at the things that you have accomplished with pride that you did the best you could. You squeezed every drop of juice out of every single moment. You saw obstacles as learning experiences so that you could make your life better for you and others. When you look back, you know that it was a life well lived.

Everybody needs a positive compelling or a negative compelling future. This is just a fancy way of saying that the thought of your future is either something that you want to stay away from or something that you want to happen.

Your future is yet to be decided. You have your own choices, and to a great degree, you are able to influence your future, but which future is going to be yours? Every single action, thought, and decision will lead you towards a positive or negative future. Which would you rather have? Until you are able to set a clear distinction between these futures and specifically map out the steps to achieve those goals, you might end up anywhere and this is what most people do.

In my own opinion, having an understanding of your own personality type, knowing the right people, money, and time are the most important resources. Given enough time and money, everybody could reach their goals, but time is limited. There is only so much time in the day.

You can gain knowledge, skills, experiences, understandings, possessions, and money, but time is the one resource that you can't control. Yet, time is the most valuable. Humans are great at wasting time. Let us count the ways:

1. Arguing with loved ones, family, and friends.
2. Mindlessly watching TV shows.
3. Aimlessly surfing the internet.
4. Wasting time on social media.
5. Traveling to work.
6. Not sleeping at night.
7. Negative thinking.
8. Surfing through junk email.
9. Handling telemarketers.

The best way to manage your time more effectively is to plan out your day in the morning or the night before and try to chunk activities into a manageable size. It also helps to stop and ask yourself questions during the day. Ask yourself what you want to be doing right now? What do I need to be doing? Things like that, to make sure that you stay on track with your goals.

To help you out with managing your time even more, here is an 18 minute time management plan.

Step 1: Set Daily Plan (5 minutes). Before you switch on your computer, grab a paper and pen and decide what is going to make your day successful. What will you be able to accomplish today that will further your goals? Write all of that down.

The most important thing here is to take out your calendar and schedule those tasks into your day. Make sure that you put the hardest task at the very beginning of the day so that you have the most energy to accomplish it. You need to decide when and where you are going to do something, otherwise, it should be removed from your list.

Step 2: Refocus (1 minute each hour). Set a timer on your watch or phone that goes off each hour. When you hear the ring, stop, take a deep breath, look at your to-do list, and see if you have spent the last hour productively. Then recommit to how you are going to spend the next hour.

Step 3: Review (5 minutes). Turn off your computer and review how your day has gone. What did you do well? Where did you lose focus? What distractions did you have?

This three-step process will help you begin and end your day on the right foot. Now, I do have one last thing for you about handling your time wisely. That is using a time management app. Todoist is on the top of the list for these types of apps. There is a free todoist or you can by $29 a year for premium todoist. The app allows you to assign your to-do list items due dates and you can sort them into different project labels. They also give you karma points when you consistently complete tasks.

There are other time management apps that can help improve your productivity as well, such as Be Focused Timer, Kiwake App, Focus Booster, and Loop – Habit Tracker. No matter what app you choose, stick with that one app. You will be amazed at how much better you manage your time.

Productivity Hack

The time has come for me to share the productivity hack that will change everything for you. This will involve creating a table of how you want your day to look and how important it is to take regular breaks.

When it comes to a daily schedule, there are two types of people:

- The minimalist who has a couple of recurring events, but a lot of free time for long periods of time.

- The overscheduler who creates calendars that look like finger painted pictures with overlapping meetings. They have their day planned out from the moment they get up.

These are both terrible for their own reasons. When you're overscheduled, you have no time for yourself. The more "in control" a person is over their calendar, the less control they feel that they have over their life. Plus, figuring out how long it is going to take to finish something is hard to estimate.

As for the minimalist, they are only living in la la land. They have likely offloaded all of their things in some way shape or form. Having a good daily schedule is the key to a successful life.

Start by creating time bookends for what is the most important work that you need to get done. Mark Twain once said that if the first thing you did in the morning was swallowed a frog, then the rest of the day would be a breeze. You want to create a time block for the most important things you need to get done.

What you don't want to do is begin your day with stress, emotional triggers, and distractions. Build recurring time into your day to accomplish what is most important before you do anything else. Your energy levels are naturally higher in the morning, and finishing something important will work like a domino effect that pushes you through your day.

Next, you can set up your complete schedule for the day instead of just the morning. This shouldn't look like the schedule of the overscheduler whose day is filled up with the priorities of others. Instead, you need to protect your time to do the things that you want to each day. This will give you the change to think about how you would like your ideal workday to look. If the way you have been spending your day isn't lining up, then you may need to re-evaluate your priorities.

Next, place your availability into the minimum amount you can, around ten to 15 minutes. With your meaningful morning and your skeleton schedule, the next thing you have to look at are the inevitable responsibilities, meetings, appointments, and tasks that will show up and screw up the day. A good schedule protects your time. So using processes that keep your time protected is a great place to start. Instead of setting meetings for 30 minutes or longer, set them for as short as possible. Try to aim for 10 to 15 minutes. Elon Musk has his day broken into five-minute chunks and the person requesting his time has to ask for more time if they need it.

Doing this, plus adding in intention open slots, will help you out for those last-minute surprises.

Next, you need to make sure that you are mindful of your flow. A good schedule will provide you with momentum and not take it away. People tend to forget their state of mind when they schedule tasks, meetings, or events. You don't want to make quick shifts from one task to the next. You need to schedule your activities in a way that flows naturally.

Next, you need to do a regular audit of your calendar to clear out dead time. Calendars aren't just for planning; they're also a great way to reflect. Every three months, take the time to look back at your schedule. Look at the time you spent on each of your projects, how you divided up your time, along with anything else that you can think of.

With all of this information, you can see if where you spent your time matches up with your intentions. If it's not, then you need to adjust your schedule.

Lastly, you have to make sure that you keep your commitments in a single place. You don't want to separate your personal and professional calendars. This will only cause troubles if you do because things are bound to overlap. Place everything on a single calendar so that you know the actual amount of time you have.

Now, you have learned how to make a good schedule, but there is another important part of this. You need to make sure that you have breaks. Have you ever been facing a problem that you couldn't figure out when you take a break, and then when you came back, you had figured out the solution? This shows the power of a break.

When you are working on something or thinking, your prefrontal cortex is at work and controls the thinking part of your brain. When you are working on goal-oriented work that you have to concentrate on, the PFC helps you to focus on your goals. PFC also controls willpower, executive functioning, and logical thinking. That's a lot of work for a little part of your brain. Here are some different ways and reasons to make sure that you take breaks during your day:

1. *Take a movement break.*

Constantly sitting places you at greater risk for developing obesity, depression, diabetes, and heart disease. Getting up every hour to take a walk or stretch will help your body and mind.

2. *You can prevent decision fatigue.*

Having to make frequent decisions during your day can wear down your reasoning and willpower. Decision fatigue can end up causing procrastination and simplistic decision-making. Try taking a 25-minute break whenever you can. This will give your brain some time to recharge.

3. *Breaks will bring back motivation for achieving your goals.*

When you have to focus on something with sustained attention, it can be fatiguing to our PFC. Taking your mind off of this can help to renew and strengthen your motivation to finish it.

4. *Take some time to connect with nature or with the city.*

Figure out if your mind needs to calm down or if it needs some excitement. If you need to calm down, then take a walk on a nature trail. If you are in need of some excitement walk, walk along the city streets to amp up your day.

5. *Switch up your environment.*

Briefly leaving your workspace and taking a walk somewhere else will allow you to switch gears and give your brain a break.

If you start to use everything you have learned about creating a schedule and making sure you take breaks, then you will be a productivity pro in no time.

Mistakes

While time management is very important, there are right and wrong ways to use it. Let's take a quick look at some of the most common mistakes people make when it comes to time management.

1. *Focusing your time on the wrong things.*

You should never let your goals slip to the wayside. Not working on the correct things is the main reason why people have trouble managing their time. In order to be productive, you have to know what you need to work on. For example, when things start getting crazy, they focus on the problem and start to blame others. The right thing for them to do is to focus on finding a solution.

2. *Trying to be perfect.*

Nobody is perfect, period. Let me repeat that again. Nobody is perfect. Don't worry about whether or not you can do it perfectly or even at all. Set your mind to what you want to do, and do it. Do it as well as you can. Don't focus on the little details right off. Start working, and those things will come.

3. *Not taking any breaks.*

I have a question for you. Do you believe that you are doing a lot of work or do you believe that you have too much time and not getting anything done? This is extremely subjective. A workaholic will likely feel that they don't have the time no matter the amount of work they put in. Somebody who isn't a workaholic may feel that they have done a lot need to rest. The point being is that you have to figure out the best balance between work and rest. You need to make sure that you take enough breaks so that you don't get burned out.

4. *Forgetting to create a to-do list.*

We've talked about the importance of to-do lists before. You have to create your to-do list so that you know what you need to do during the day. If you don't have a clear plan as to what you need to do, then you won't get anything accomplished.

5. *Getting a late start to your day.*

Most every successful person will start their days early. Howard Schultz, the man behind Starbucks, gets up at 4:30. Richard Branson gets up at 5:45. Tim Cook gets up at 4:30. When you get up early, you have time to jump-start your day and accomplish things that you normally don't get done.

Morning Routine (Make This a Habit for True Success)

Everybody is different. We all live different lives and we all have different goals. The one thing that we all need to do, though, is to plan out our day before it begins. The best thing you can do is to write out your to-do list for the next day. We're going to look at creating your morning routine to help you get your day started right.

It's tough being a morning person when you aren't one naturally. It takes a lot of discipline to get into the habit of waking up earlier. But creating a productive earlier morning routine could be what's standing between you and your goals. Think about these statements for a minute to see how many resonate with you:

- I went to be late, so I had to sleep later.
- I meant to get up early until the morning got here.
- I have too much going on at home in the morning and I don't have time for me, so why bother?
- I know what I need to do, but I don't have the willpower.

If you notice that you are nodding your head with these statements, then you're going to love this section.

What is the importance of creating a morning routine?

At the basic level, it will get rid of procrastination, be happier, healthier, and create success for your day. Think about this, how different would life be like if you were happier? The American Psychological Association performed a study that discovered following a morning routine would reduce your anxiety and depression. It causes your to-do list to seem less daunting.

But I hate mornings!

If you really hate mornings, the benefits may still now be swaying you in the direction of a morning routine. You may even be thinking that you hate them so much that there is no way that this could ever change. Guess what, you can do whatever you want. The key to creating a successful morning routine is your mind. You have to overcome the "I'm not a morning person" thought process. So if you continue to tell yourself that, your mind will make sure that it remains true.

Think back to the last time that you tried to get up earlier on a regular basis. To start, your motivation was probably high and you were ready to tackle everything. You went to bed earlier and set an alarm to wake you up at dawn. You were full of confidence for the next day. This probably worked for a couple of days.

However, the day came when the alarm hit off and you had no motivation. You hit the snooze button and stayed in bed because you were certain that today wasn't your day.

Don't worry, though, there is some good news. Motivation can become more permanent. There is no need to be motivated to do something because taking action will create motivation. There is a five-step process you can take to make sure you stick with your morning routine: reminder, routine, reward, rehearse, and record.

First, remind yourself of your morning routine.

Second, figure out the routine you want to do, meaning, what things you want to do during your morning routine.

Third, figure out the rewards that come along with your morning routine.

Fourth, rehearse successfully completing your habit.

Last, record your morning routine on your calendar once you finish it so that you watch yourself progress.

Alright, so the snooze button causes a lot of problems. If that is your first action when you hear the alarm, you are beginning the day with procrastination. You are telling your subconscious that you don't have enough self-discipline to even get out of the bed.

If you are one to pick up your phone and check social media and email first thing, you are placing other people's lives ahead of yours. You want to use your morning to focus on you. Hold off on checking your phone.

The key to making sure that you wake up in the next morning ready to kill the day is to make sure that you get a good night's sleep. Chances are, your mind is getting in the way of your sleep. Try a few of these things to silence your mind:

- Keep a journal and write out the things that stress you out to release them.

- Take a few minutes to practice some mindful breathing so that you can live in the present and not in the past or future.

- Quiet your inner voice and release it of any worries.

- Look back at the good things that you have experienced during your day, which will help your mind see everything that is right in your life while allowing you to release the little hiccups you may have experienced.

- Look forward to the great night's sleep that you are going to get.

The goals are to get your body ready for sleep, so make sure you don't eat a lot before bed or your digestive system is going to keep you up. Try to limit your alcohol intake. Too much may help you get to sleep, but the sleep won't be quality sleep. Plus, you may wake up with a hangover.

I know we're talking about morning routines, but having a bedtime routine may help you to get yourself ready for the next morning. It may be helpful to pick out the clothes you are going to wear the next day, that way it is one less thing that you have to think about. While you're at it, you can also grab your workout clothes as well.

Once you have everything together for your morning, you can do some fun things that will relax you. This could be listening to soothing music, taking a bath, or reading a book. You can do anything as long as it helps to calm you down. It could be tempting to use this time to go through your email or watch TV, but it is best if you can take the last hour before sleep to shut off electronic devices.

There are some things you can do to your environment to ensure you sleep well.

- Move your alarm so that you can't see the time. This will keep the glow and the time from keeping you awake. You may even want to place it on the other side of your room so that you have to get out of bed to shut it off in the morning.

- You could also make your bedroom a "device-free zone" and make sure all of your devices are in another space in your house. You could also just turn them off.

- Purchase a pet bed so that your pets won't bother you as much. (This tip is subjective to the pet. It doesn't work for all animals.)

- Try to keep the temperature of your bedroom around 65 degrees Fahrenheit. This is the ideal temp according to the National Sleep Foundation.

- Use blackout curtains to block out outside lights. This is especially important if there are street lights near your house or if you are located at the end of the road where you may have headlines shining through your windows.

Basically, you want to make your bedroom so soothing that it lulls you to sleep so that you wake up feeling great and rejuvenated.

Steps for Success

Now we're going to create you a morning routine. You can, of course, change this up a bit to suit you. You can also add things to it if you want.

1. *Hydrate*

The first thing you are going to do when you get up in the morning is to drink a glass of ice cold water. Of course, any other business you need to do before this you can, but the first action of your routine is drinking a glass of cold water.

This glass of water will help you to wake up, and the fact that it's cold will help even more. Whether you choose to drink cold water or room temp water doesn't matter, though. Drinking a glass of water first thing in the morning will improve your day no matter its temperature.

It helps to increase nutrient absorption by purifying the colon so that your body has an easier job of absorbing the important parts of food. Early morning water consumption will increase your daily blood and muscle cells. Water also boosts your metabolism, helps to moisturize and clear your skin, and balances out your lymph system.

2. *Breathing exercises*

After your glass of water, you're going to take some time to ground yourself through breathing exercises. Basically, you are going to take a few minutes to meditate and focus on the present moment and not the past or future. Performing breathing exercises each morning will reduce depression and anxiety, improve energy, increase relaxation, decrease stress, improve the immune system, and improve mental concentration.

This should only take you about five to ten minutes. It's a good idea before you start to blow your nose and to have tissues handy just in case you need them. Don't strain yourself and make sure you won't be distracted. If you start to feel anxious, stop the exercise. Lastly, begin slowly.

Here is an easy breathing exercise to try:

- Place a hand on your stomach and relax the abs muscles.

- Slowly breathe in through your nose and the bottoms of your lungs to fill with air. Your hand should move as your stomach rises.

- With this same inhale, feel the rib cage move out as the air starts to move up until your collar bones move.

- Hold the breath for a moment, and then breathe out through your mouth, gently releasing the air from the top all the way to the bottom of the lungs.

- At the end of the breath, pull your belly into your spine, pushing out all the air that is left inside.

3. Exercise

The next thing you will need to do is a workout. This can be any workout that you want to do. The important thing is to get your heart rate up for about 20 minutes.

While the important thing is just to make sure that you work out each day, doing so in the morning comes with its own added benefits. First off, you will end up consuming fewer calories. Brigham Young University discovered that morning exercise can make food less appealing.

It will set you up for more activity during the day. That means you will have more energy to accomplish the things that you need to. Your blood pressure will also be lower, by around 10%. When it comes around to night again, you will find that you sleep better. Evening exercises can leave your body too revved up for you to relax to get to sleep.

Cardio exercise is the best, so a good run, bike ride, swim, or even dancing are all great exercises to do first thing in the morning.

4. Visualize

The next step in your morning routine is visualization. You will take a few minutes to sit and visualize how you want your life to look. This practice will activate your subconscious mind so that you can generate creativity to achieve your goals. It will also help to program your brain so that it can recognize the resources that you need to reach your dreams.

This visualization doesn't have to be difficult. All you have to do is sit for a few moments and picture what you want your life to be. Be thorough when you do this. Think about every part of your life and what you would like to see.

5. Look at your goals

Once your visualization is done, you will look over your short and long-term goals. Take a look back at everything you have written down to refresh yourself. This will ensure that you know exactly what you need to be working towards.

6. Plan your day

Now, you will sit down and create your schedule for the day. You can either do a simple to-do list or create a full schedule. A schedule will help you be more accountable and may make your day easier. A schedule will show what you need to do at what time so that you don't feel overwhelmed by a list of to-dos.

7. Gratitude

The last thing you need to do before starting your day is to be grateful. During this time, you will write down things that you are thankful for. This will remind you of the good things in life so that you don't get caught up in the dwelling of the rough times. Be grateful for where you are currently and all of the opportunities you have. You are able to work through any task that you are presented with and you can reach every goal that you want to.

So many times, people start their days focused on the negative. Didn't get enough sleep. Not enough fruit for a smoothie. Favorite outfit is dirty. And the list goes on. This creates a bad day. You go around feeling like you're worthless and this leads to less productivity. Gratitude will help to pull you out of this problem.

Now, there are two ways you can do this. You can create a gratitude jar or write in a gratitude journal. Keeping either one of these brings about huge changes in your life. Practicing gratitude helps improve your sleep, keeps you from getting sick, and makes you happier.

For a gratitude journal, all you need to do is write down five things that you are grateful for. This can be anything and they only have to be a single sentence. But it's best if you take the time to really dig into the process. In order to make sure that you do experience the benefits of gratitude you have to:

- Don't just do it to do it. It works better if you go into this with the want to become happier and grateful.

- Try to go deep instead of listing out more. It's best to really explain the things you are grateful for instead of having a list of ten or more.

- It helps if you focus on the people who you are grateful for because it has a greater impact on you than things.

- Try subtraction. Instead of thinking about how things have helped your life, write about how your life would be without certain things.

- Write down things that were surprising or unexpected.

So, for a journal, you will write out some things that you are grateful for. If you want to create a jar, all you need is a jar and some scraps of paper. Write things you are grateful for on a piece of paper and put it into the jar. These are both great options, you can also look back over them any time you are feeling down. They can help to lift your spirits back up.

That's it for your morning routine. Do this every morning and you will notice that you have morning energy and you will get more things done.

The Truth about Productivity and Self-Esteem That No One Has Told You

Productivity and self-esteem work hand in hand. Both of these will come naturally the more you follow the steps that we have covered. Once you have reached a comfortable place with what you want in life and you start to create habits, then you will be set up for true confidence and happiness. But in case you're not positive about this happening, let's take a look at the relationship between productivity and self-esteem.

Have you met a person who has ever grown an oak tree from a pumpkin seed? Probably not, because the one thing that I am certain of is the law of nature, which is that you reap what you sow. Everybody is probably thinking, "Well, yeah." But the problem is that people don't really understand this because so many people try to get something for nothing.

No matter who you are, you would love to get everything you desire for free. People want more, but they don't want to put the effort into getting what they want. People don't understand value creation.

Value creation isn't you going to work at eight and going home at five. What you do between those times is what's important. For example, if you arrived late, ate breakfast at work, chatted with friends about what happened over the weekend, spent a few hours scrolling through Facebook, took a bunch of bathroom breaks, stayed at lunch longer than you were supposed to, and then shut down before the day was over, you would be subtracting value from your day.

There are studies who have found that most workers are only 50% productive at work. This is a waste of time. 35% of your life is typically spent at work. Think about this. How do you make more money? To make more money, you have to be productive.

Everything you do needs to be to the best of your abilities. Adding value to your work means that you find solutions to your problems, develop something new that you have always wanted to, and do things faster and accurately.

To know if you're adding value by being productive, write down five to ten successes you have reached by the end of the day. This will really show you how you are spending your time and put your life in perspective.

The main reason why people subtract value from their life is due to low self-esteem. Everybody views their self like a certain image, probably different than how others view them. This image you have about yourself impacts how you feel about yourself and how much value you place on yourself. Self-esteem can be changed though.

Looking for the positive, good, or learning experiences in things that you have done is a good place to start when it comes to improving your self-esteem. This is just another habit that you can create. People who are negative are more likely to have low self-esteem because they live on the bad things and the mistakes. They make their self feel useless even though they may have done a lot of good during the day.

When you start to realize that low self-esteem causes the majority of people's problems, you will start to see the issues of resistance to change, poor performance, and low productivity.

People who cultivate high self-esteem will succeed more in their personal and professional life. They are willing to put in the time and effort to reach their accomplishments. Let's dig a little deeper on this.

Whether you are working on your personal goals or working on a larger company goal, the only way you are going to achieve anything is to take action. This action needs to also be of quality and quantity. But, if you suffer from low self-esteem, you will sabotage your efforts without realizing it.

You've probably met people who are skilled and knowledgeable in their chosen field, yet their work always falls short of their potential. This happens because they don't believe in their self, or they believe in their abilities but they don't think they are worthy of success.

What's worse, is that people with low self-esteem don't think that they are worthy for great results so they will "dumb down" the things they do so that they don't stand out and won't get noticed. When you have a poor perception of your competency and abilities, you are setting yourself up to fail or reach mediocrity.

There is a strong relationship between lack of belief in worthiness and lack of belief in capability. Those who think they are competent but not worthy may end up being boastful. This ends up backfiring when their accomplishments don't match their claims. Resume padding is a common example of this problem.

Those who view their self as worthy but actually lack the competency will blame everybody else and everything else for their lack of results. They don't take responsibility. These people normally speak like they are self-important, but their results still don't back up their words. In both of these cases, people will quit trusting them.

We're going to take a look at an NLP technique that can help you to boost your self-esteem to make sure that you stay productive. But, I also want to remind you that your self-esteem and productivity will improve on their own if you follow the other things that we have covered as well.

It's a good idea to do this ten step exercise once or twice a day when you feel like you're struggling with low self-esteem. Doing this first thing in the morning is a good idea so that you can start your day on the right foot. Only through consistent practice will you be able to develop the habits that will improve your self-esteem when faced with everyday challenges.

1. *Imagine and relax*

Start by shutting your eyes and allow your body to relax. Take a few deep breaths. Now, take your attention to a person who you know genuinely loves and cares about you. Picture them in your mind and fully experience their radiance.

2. *Imagine you're writing*

Picture yourself at a desk in a magical room full of paintings and ornaments. You're sitting in a comfy chair with a pen in your hand and writing out your biography. You're writing out everything in your life and the way it has unfolded thus far. This includes the good and the bad. This story covers your past, present, and the unwritten future that you are fitting together.

As you write, you realize that the loving person you thought of earlier is standing on the other side of a glass door. They are observing you just like a guardian angel.

3. *Continue to write and feel*

As you look at that person, you start to write out some notes about their place in your story. You talk about their features, virtues, and qualities in detail. You also start to think about the amazing times the two of you have had together. You take a moment to think: How do I feel when around them? How do they make me feel about myself? How do they make me better?

As you think about these things, you experience a shock of confidence coursing through you, leaving you inspired and invigorated.

4. *Feel and Float*

You observe this person smiling at you. Their smile is warm and inviting and makes your heart happy. You are slowly drawn closer to them. In fact, part of you floats to stand with them. Both of you are standing there observing you write about your life.

5. *Look at yourself*

As you stand with your friend and watch yourself sit at the desk and write, you start to reflect on your thoughts and feelings. How do I look from this point of view? How do I feel about myself? What am I capable of achieving? What things could this person do in their life? You think about these things as you continue to watch yourself write.

6. *Become the loving person*

You turn toward the loving person. You take their hand with a smile and are pulled inside of them. You can see things now through their eyes, listen with their ears, and feel with their heart. You aren't you anymore. You are now a part of the loving person who loves you dearly.

7. *Change of perspective*

As you view yourself from this other person's perspective, you start to consider, think, and observe the way they see you. You ask: What do they think of me? How do they feel about me? What qualities do they see in me? What do they think I can achieve?

Don't question or judge the answers that come to mind. You stay mindful of these answers and you are filled with positive and warm energy coming from your loved one.

8. *Transfer their perspective*

Feeling as you do towards yourself, you start to detach your awareness away from the loving person. As you detach yourself, you move the emotions, perspective, and feelings that they have toward you back into your body sitting at the desk. As this happens, you will find yourself writing the feelings you are experiencing. You highlight the way that you feel and how it has changed your perspective about yourself and your world.

9. *Write the future*

You can now take the positive feelings and start to write out your future with a sense of appreciation. You ask yourself: How do I now feel about myself? What am I capable of? What kind of future can I create for myself? What fears can I overcome? What challenges can I tackle? How can I act with more confidence?

Reflect completely on each of these questions. You think about the impact that this is having on you and commit yourself to add positivity to everything that you do.

10. Awaken empowerment

As you finish up your story, the magical room begins to fade away. As it fades, you start to slowly return to the physical you. You are now back in the present. As you open your eyes, you feel positivity coursing through your body. You feel empowered. Everything seems possible. You ask: What's possible now? What can I achieve from this new perspective? What can I do to make my day extraordinary?

The answers you give these questions will help you to create the foundation for your life. Make sure that you remain consistent and don't ever give up with this practice and all the other practices that we have covered.

30-Day Challenge

We've made it to the end. Now the time has come for your 30-day challenge. Everything that I will ask you to do will help you with everything that we have talked about. Don't get frustrated if you feel like you aren't doing things right. As long as you do the best that you can, then you are doing it right. There are six things that I want you to do every morning, so make sure you take note and do them every day. Each day will have a separate action you will need to take. Your six daily actions are:

- Get up before 8 AM.

- First thing in the morning, do 50 pushups, 50 sit ups, and 50 squats.

- Take a cold shower. You take your shower like normal with the water warm and then shock yourself at the end with cold water.

- Perform one task that will help you reach your life goal.

- Do 20 minutes of exercising, preferably a session of running, bike ride, and skipping rope.

- Do not snack during the day.

Let's get started.

Day One

Today's special challenge is to commit. I want you to set a goal for what you want to accomplish during this 30-day challenge. You really need to challenge yourself so that you pull yourself out of your comfort zone. You can't choose to do something that you already do on a daily basis. You can also choose three bonus goals if you would like, but your main focus should be the first goal that is of the highest priority to you. Remember, your goal should be whatever you want. Maybe you want to write a book, so now you are going to actually sit down and write that book. You could want to learn how to cook a gourmet meal. Whatever it is, write it down and commit to reaching that goal in 30-days.

Day Two

Today you are going to declutter and organize. This can be physical clutter, work-desk spilling over with papers, computer filled with icons, or an inbox full of emails. To reach stress-free productivity, you need to declutter your environment. Clutter causes negative side effects to your focus and how you process information so get rid of it.

Day Three

Today you will focus and make things happen. You want to create a habit of working on your goals daily. The main reason why people don't accomplish things is that they let other stuff get in their way. I want you to schedule time for accomplishing your goals. Create an actual schedule and set reminders to make sure you don't forget to focus.

Day Four

Tonight I want you to take five to ten minutes to plan out what you are going to do tomorrow. As you sleep, your subconscious mind will work on the things you need to do. You will wake up the next morning having already figure out how to fix your problems.

Day Five

Today I want you to reward yourself. Sit down and think about different ways you could reward yourself for accomplishing things. Your rewards can be anything except for food item.

Day Six

Today you are going to review your productivity. Look back at the last five days and see what you have done well and what you can do better in the next week.

Day Seven

Today I want you to re-energize yourself by eating healthy. Pick foods that will help to cleanse your body as well.

Day Eight

Today you are going to schedule and prioritize the week ahead. Plan out the things that you want to accomplish in the coming week and create your reminders.

Day Nine

Today you are going to take action and get things done. Stop procrastinating and get to work.

Day Ten

Today you want to stay in the flow. Celebrate your success so that you feel happy for what you have accomplished, but keep a sense of urgency so that you continue to work towards your goals.

Day Eleven

Today I want you to work on self-discipline. You will find days where achieving your goals are easy and then there will be somewhere they aren't. You have to cultivate self-discipline to make it through the tough days.

Day Twelve

Today I want you to accept responsibility for your life. This means that you focus on the things that you can control and quit worrying about things that you can't.

Day Thirteen

Today you are going to solve problems. Problems are going to arise, but it's the way that you handle them that counts. Instead of focusing on the problem, look for the solution.

Day Fourteen

Today you are going to take some breaks. This doesn't mean you get the day off. You just get to add in some more time to recharge. This is something you should have been doing a bit of all along, but just in case, you now have permission to do so. Don't take too long of a break though, you don't want to lose momentum.

Day Fifteen

Today you are going to reassess things. The middle tends to be the trickiest part of all. To work through this slump, I want you to reassess your goals and remind yourself of the reason why you are doing this.

Day Sixteen

Today I want you to make sure that you are proactive with your happiness. It's important that you stay excited with what you do.

Day Seventeen

Today you are going to simplify by saying no. You have to say no sometimes to make sure that you achieve your goals. Being a yes man won't serve your best interests.

Day Eighteen

Today you are going to get rid of distractions. Turn off the TV, your phone, stop checking Facebook, or your email. Focus solely on what you need to get done.

Day Nineteen

Today you're not doing anything new, just make sure you stick to what you are supposed to do.

Day Twenty

Today I want you to think of your big picture and take small steps to get to it. It's a lot easy to write a couple hundred words in a day than 4000.

Day Twenty-One

Today I want you to look at your strengths. Look at what people praise you for and what you are most passionate about.

Day Twenty-Two

Today I want you to remind yourself that you don't need to be perfect. It's more important to do things than to be perfect.

Day Twenty-Three

Today I want you to switch up your environment. Do some of your tasks in a new place if you can. A change of scenery could provide you with new inspiration.

Day Twenty-Four

Today I want you to make sure that you remain motivated for this last week. Think about what would happen if you stopped and what would happen if you finished these 30-days. Which option would be better for you?

Day Twenty-Five

Today I want you to look at your energy levels. Figure out the times of the day where you have the most energy and adjust your tasks accordingly.

Day Twenty-Six

Today I want you to drink more water. Often people will forget to drink water and it is so important, so drink more water.

Day Twenty-Seven

Today is a day to focus on your tasks at hand. Go get things done.

Day Twenty-Eight

Today you are creating lasting habits. You have stuck to your goal for 28 days now, so you probably won't ever stop them.

Day Twenty-Nine

Today I want you to be grateful for how far you have come. Look back at the things that you have accomplished.

Day Thirty

Today, I want you to look over what you have done these last 30 days see how you have performed.

You've reached the end. I hope the challenge proved helpful and that you will stick with your new habits.

Conclusion

Thank you for making it through to the end of *NLP Productivity*, let's hope it was informative and able to provide you with all of the tools you need to achieve your goals whatever they may be.

You've learned a lot and it's okay if you feel a bit overwhelmed. The important thing is that you review what you have learned and start taking inspired action towards improving your life. Remember, the first thing you need to do is figure out exactly what you want in life. This means in your life, job, and family. You are living for yourself and nobody else, so make sure it's what you want and not what you think you should do.

With that in mind, you can start to use the NLP techniques that we have covered to improve your life ten-fold. Keep in mind that NLP is only part of the puzzle. You can also make changes to other areas of your life as well. Remember the foods that can help you increase your energy, as well as making sure that you get regular exercise.

You also have to make sure that you actually sit down and create your goals. Nothing is going to get done if you don't know what you need to do. Remember, don't let yourself get overwhelmed by your long-term goals, break them down into small and manageable pieces.

While learning all of this is fine and dandy, you still actually have to get started doing something. You have to create the self-discipline you need to achieve the things that you want in life. Create the habits that you know will help you in the long-term and stick to them. Don't let yourself fall back into bad habits.

None of this will get done if you don't start changing your time management skills. This is something that everybody struggles with. So many people will say, there are just not enough hours in the day, yet everybody has the same 24-hours. Those who know how to use those hours to their advantage are the ones who accomplish their dreams.

The fun part comes when you start putting all of these things together to create a new routine. As soon as you can, start implementing the morning routine that we covered. Make sure that you plan out your day so that you don't have any excuses. Also, get started on the 30-day challenge. It's fun and challenging, but it will help you to achieve everything that we have covered. The important thing is that you get started.

Finally, if you found this book useful in any way, a review on Amazon is always appreciated!

Accelerated Learning

Master Memory Improvement, Be Productive and Declutter Your Mind To Boost Your IQ Through Insane Focus, Unlimited Memory, Photographic Memory, Speed Reading, and Mindfulness

Adam Hunter

© Copyright 2018 - All rights reserved

The following eBook is reproduced below with the goal of providing information that is as accurate and reliable as possible. Regardless, purchasing this eBook can be seen as consent to the fact that both the publisher and the author of this book are in no way experts on the topics discussed within and that any recommendations or suggestions that are made herein are for entertainment purposes only. Professionals should be consulted as needed prior to undertaking any of the action endorsed herein.

This declaration is deemed fair and valid by both the American Bar Association and the Committee of Publishers Association and is legally binding throughout the United States.

Furthermore, the transmission, duplication, or reproduction of any of the following work including specific information will be considered an illegal act irrespective of if it is done electronically or in print. This extends to creating a secondary or tertiary copy of the work or a recorded copy and is only allowed with the express written consent from the Publisher. All additional right reserved.

The information in the following pages is broadly considered a truthful and accurate account of facts and as such, any inattention, use, or misuse of the information in question by the reader will render any resulting actions solely under their purview. There are no scenarios in which the publisher or the original author of this work can be in any fashion deemed liable for any hardship or damages that may befall them after undertaking information described herein.

Additionally, the information in the following pages is intended only for informational purposes and should thus be thought of as universal. As befitting its nature, it is presented without assurance regarding its prolonged validity or interim quality. Trademarks that are mentioned are done without written consent and can in no way be considered an endorsement from the trademark holder.

Introduction

Memory and learning, as I'm sure you know, are important to everything you do in life. That's why you are here. The information you are going to learn can be helpful in many different areas of life. You can use this information to help you learn a new language, learn new things in a shorter time period, prepare for a test, remember names, and a whole host of things. The key is tapping into your memory.

Centuries ago, our ancestors saw memorization as a prized skill. They passed cultures down through the years by remembering laws, taboos, history, legends, and stories. Then, when the printing press was created, people started to "look things up," instead of remembering them. Today, we have Google and the internet, which is pretty much preventing us from using our memory. What we can't remember, all we have to do is look it up.

Teachers don't require their students to memorize multiplication tables, famous speeches, poems, and many other types of academic material as often today. These things used to be ingrained in students' minds. The disdain for memorization grew along with other intellectually damaging effects of the post-modern world. Now, education focuses on hands-on activities, inquiry learning, critical thinking, new math, among other things. These new emphases are important, except they don't allow children to learn how to memorize things. This has created mentally lazy people. This is no fault of their own, it just happened. This can be remedied and should be because mental laziness isn't going to allow you to succeed.

Memorization disciplines your mind. When you have a lazy mind, it can cause you to be easily distracted, think very little about things, or you think in a sloppy manner. Memorization will train your mind to be industrious and remain focused.

There will be times where you can't just "Google it." You may not have access to the internet, or your phone could be dead. Not everything is available on the internet, either. There is a great deal of irrelevant information that you will find when you search for things as well. There are also times when looking things up isn't helpful in certain situations, like when you are learning to use a foreign language, when you are asked to make an impromptu speech, or when you want to be an expert on a subject.

Memorization will also create the things that we think about. Nobody is able to think when they are in a vacuum of information. In order to be an expert on anything, you have to have knowledge about it.

People think using the ideas that working memory holds onto, which is only able to be accessed quickly from their stored memory. Understanding things is improved by the information that you have in your working memory. Without this kind of knowledge, you will experience a mind full of mush.

The muscles that you use when you memorize things develop learning and improve your ability to learn. The more that you are able to remember, the more you will be able to learn.

History shows us that great minds and full of knowledge. Picasso had to have an understanding of how to paint before you picked up a brush and began to paint something. Einstein had to have a good understanding of the physics of his time before he was able to see the errors within it. Plato had to have a good understanding of Greek philosophy before he was able to find his Academy in North Athens. Steve Jobs had to have a good understanding of programming before he created Apple.

If you are interested in learning more, you have to go back to the basics that have worked for people in the past. What people have been doing isn't working. The fundamental skill that people forget about is memorization.

Memorization is only the start of accelerated learning, though. The next important thing is focus. Focus and memory work hand in hand. You can't memorize things if you aren't focused, and you can't focus on something unless you are able to access memorized information.

But why is focus so important? When you are focused on one thing for a certain time period you will do better work, get more done quicker, and your creativity will be improved. Staying focused on one thing at a time is also less stressful on your mind. When you are less stressed, you will be happier.

To be focused means that you have created clear goals and objectives. You work towards reaching those goals and objectives. When you try to figure out what you are going to do, you base your decision on what you need to do in order to progress towards your goals with the resources and time that you have available.

When you are focused on the present, you are only focused on the activity that you need to complete. Anything else that is going on isn't important, so you remove distractions so that you give the task at hand you full and undivided attention.

The alternative to being focused is doing a bunch of other things, jumping from task to task without completely finishing something. Those who aren't focused normally spend their time doing anything but what they need to get done. What they choose to do is often dictated by:

- What makes them feel busier
- What feels easier
- Bullies who tell them what to do
- Another person's priorities
- Urgency

Think about multitasking where people believe they are getting a lot done, but they are working slower and at a lower standard. Over and over, research has found that multitasking isn't possible and serves no purpose. Staying focused and finishing a single task at a time before going to something else is more effective.

There are a lot of different reasons why people find it hard to remain focused. One thing is for sure, we live in a world where we are constantly being distracted by social media, internet, cell phones, radio, TV, as well as more people that live closer together.

Not only that, but we live in a consumerist economy. So many different entities depend on us spending more money so that they can make more money. This means that we are faced with more disruptions in the way of billboards, neon signs, mail, phone calls, and emails to push marketing in our face. It's hard to take a quiet stroll in the park without noticing some sort of advertisement.

It's hard to get rid of all of our distractions. The best way to do so is to find a room where you can shut the door and turn off all electronics that you can and turn off notifications, but even still, if you let anybody know where you are, they could easily distract you.

The benefits of being focused are endless. First off, tasks get finished faster than if you are trying to finish two or more things. Let's say you are trying to take an online Spanish course, do your homework for another class, and research information more an upcoming paper. That list sounds stressful; now imagine jumping from task to task. The best thing to do is set everything aside except one of them.

When you turn your attention to one task, you can finish it with fewer mistakes. That means your work is going to be higher quality. Also, your creativity will kick in, which will allow you to come up with new ideas. This is perfect for a person who creates things, like musicians, writers, photographers, artists, as well as, researchers, teachers, or anybody who needs ideas.

When you are constantly connected and have to work through distractions, it will affect your stress levels and productivity.

Without focus, you don't get a lot of things done. This will cause you to fall behind, which adds even more stress. It's sometimes hard to figure out what you should be doing and what you shouldn't when you have a lot on your plate. Look at what you need to do. Is there any work that:

- Should be automated
- Should be outsourced
- Should be delegated
- Should be done by another person
- Or, shouldn't be done at all

It's easy to take on too much, which just causes more stress.

When you focus on something, you will use your subconscious mind. Think back to when you learned to ride a bike. At first, it was hard. When you started focusing on the things you were doing, the subconscious took over and help you to learn. This is true for your tasks you do every day. When of focus on one thing, your subconscious will be able to kick in help you finish it.

While you are working on one part of it, your subconscious will work on another part. You will notice when you continue on with a task that you don't have to think about it as much. This is where memory also comes in as well. Your subconscious will only work if you have something memorized about a topic.

It's easy to forget the importance of memory and focus in this day and age. With the information we are going to cover, you will learn how to re-engage your mind to improve your life.

Covering the Basics (Insane Focus)

To really get into unlocking improved learning and memory, you have to understand a few basic things about the mind.

Kill Multi-Tasking

We've already talked about how problematic multitasking is, but studies have even found that it can kill your performance and could end up hurting the brain. A study performed at Stanford University found that multitasking is less productive than focusing on a single task at a time. They also found that those who regularly bombarded their self with streams of outside information aren't able to pay attention, switch between tasks efficiently, or recall information as well as those who work on a single task.

They even went so far as to test those who believe that multitasking is a special skill. They compared groups of people based on how often they multitasked and their belief that it could improve their performance. They discovered that the heavy multitaskers were worse at multitasking than the people who focused on one thing. They performed worse because they could organize their thoughts and filter out things that were irrelevant, and they were slower when it came to switching to a different task.

Research has also found that besides slowing your down, multitasking lowers the IQ. A study at the University of London discovered that people who multitasked while performing cognitive tasks had their IQ scores decline by a similar amount to staying up all night. Men who multitasked had a 15 point drop, placing them in an average range of eight-year-olds.

So, when you find yourself typing up a report while in a business meeting, remember that your cognitive skills are being hurt so much so that you may as well have an eight-year-old write that report for you.

Not only will it affect your IQ, but it could cause permanent cognitive impairment. A study at the University of Sussex compared the time that people spend on multiple devices to MRI brain scans. They discovered that heavy multitaskers had decreased brain density in their anterior cingulate cortex. This is the region of the brain that is responsible for empathy as well as emotional and cognitive control. While there needs to be more research to figure out if multitasking is indeed physically damaging to the brain, it's clear that it has a lot of negative side effects.

If you tend to multitask, it's something that you don't want to indulge in often. Even if it doesn't create permanent brain damage, it will fuel existing difficulties you have with attention to detail, organization, and concentration. Multitasking also indicated low social and self-awareness, which are two emotional intelligence skills that are important for success at work. When you multitask, you are not only harming your performance at that moment; you could be damaging a part of your brain that is important for future success.

Focus on One Thing

Knowing what we know about multitasking, the only other option is to focus on one thing at a time. While there may be some that would still argue that doing more faster is the best path to productivity, I would argue that they're wrong. While you may be busier, you aren't being productive.

The attention we have to give what we need to work on is limited. The mind can only focus on so many things, so we need to invest our attention wisely. Single-tasking is the opposite of multitasking, and it is so much better in every way imaginable. The brain will likely resist this because it isn't as stimulating as multitasking. But when we work on a single task, it allows us to dive deeper and do better work. You won't be forced to spread your time, energy, and attention across several things at one time. Single-tasking creates attentional space around our work. This allows us to think deeper, create connections, work creatively, and find more meaning.

Take a moment to think back to the last time you were crazy-productive. Chances are, you weren't doing a million different things. You were probably working on one thing, and spending all of your energy, time, and attention on that one item. While it is going to take you some energy and time to adapt to being less stimulated during your day, you can easily see why it's worth it.

Single-tasking also increases our "attention muscles." This is how much control we have over our attention. Harvard psychologists Daniel Gillbert and Matthew Killingsworth found that 47% of our waking hours are used thinking about things that are completely unrelated to what is in front of us. The ramifications are huge: a person who is attentive 75% of the time will be more productive than a person who focuses on their work 50% of the time. When we single-task, we build our attention muscles because we have to constantly rein in our attention.

Don't believe me? Try single-tasking for the next week. Set yourself a 20-minute timer, and take that time to focus on a single task. At first, your brain will resist this, but once you get into the groove of it, you will feel amazing. Afterward, think about what you were able to accomplish in 20 minutes.

Productivity and being busy are two unrelated things. Instead, productivity and what you accomplish is what you should look at.

Be Present

With all the work and things going through our minds, it's easy to start feeling stressed and overwhelmed. This is because we are trying to store too much in short-term memory. Multitasking tends to be to blame for this as well. By dumping all of our thoughts and to-do lists into our short-term, we cause an endless information loop that we can't quit thinking about. We constantly feel like we have forgotten something.

It's like we have a hamster in our mind running endlessly on its wheel but getting absolutely nowhere. It causes us to feel physically and mentally exhausted. The mind has an amazing ability to remember unfinished tasks. This is what is called the Zeigarnik Effect. We have a "reminder system" built-in our minds. This can be useful at times, but in our modern world, it doesn't work all that well so we get overloaded. And then we can't get those thoughts out of our mind

The secret to fixing this problem is simple. We have to get this stuff out of our mind. All of those reminders and ideas need to be placed in a reliable system that will watch out for the information until the time comes where we can deal with it all. We need a way to be present at the moment, and make sure that your mind is clear.

The first thing you need to do is capture your thoughts and get them into your systems as quickly as possible. This can be a notebook that you keep with you, or you can use a free app. It doesn't matter what you do, as long as it will be something that you always have with you.

Then you have to create a daily reminder to look over the thoughts that you have captured and figure out what you are going to do. Google Calendar can send you a message on certain times to remind you to do this. When you get the reminder, you will go through the information you wrote down and figure out what you are going to do with the items. You will decide one of four things for each of the items:

- Delete – the item isn't serving any purpose and doesn't need to be done.

- Delegate – somebody else could do this.

- Defer – this can be done later.

- Do – this something I need to finish now.

That's it. When you do this on a regular basis, it will clear out your mind and allow you to focus on the task at hand. You will be more present, and you won't have to deal with your mind clutter anymore.

Imagination

The last basic you need to understand is the power of your imagination. Imagination influences everything we do. It is what creates elaborate inventions, dreams, and theories in every profession. Ultimately, imagination will influence all that we do no matter our profession.

I want you to take a moment and think about how you could use your imagination in a more deliberate and effective manner. How could you improve your personal and professional if you started to use your brain in ways that you haven't ever before?

There is nothing shameful or childish about making imagination as part of your everyday life. The more that you use your imagination, the stronger it will become. You will be amazed as you use your imagination and tap into an amazing source of infinite possibilities.

The one thing that every successful person has in common is how they use their imagination. Take, for example, Bill Gates and Steve Jobs. They imagined how personal computers could change the world, how they work, how it could teach children, and how it could entertain people.

Imagination isn't just helpful when it comes to envisioning the future. It's also helpful when it comes to learning and remembering things. Our sense of sight has evolved to become one of our strongest senses, so it's only natural that our mind likes to see things in order to remember them.

That's why you will find the majority of our memory techniques will use your imagination and mental images. The problem is, people have been conditioned to believe that imagination is inferior to logical reasoning. They think it's something that only children should do.

With these beliefs, it causes potential great ideas and learning abilities to be smothered, stifled, or killed. It also shows a lack of understanding about how important imagination is in human life.

Unlimited Memory

For our bodies to stay healthy, it's important that we exercise. So why do people not apply the same information to their brain? In order for our memory to improve, we have to train the brain, but this isn't something that has to be time-consuming and strenuous like a workout at the gym. Memory champions and psychologist both agree that the key to a better memory is visualization, and the crazier it is, the better.

Mnemonics are memory techniques that make complicated information easier to remember. The ones that tend to work the best are often rather unusual because the strange parts of life normally are more memorable than the boring ones. One study found that people remembered more information when it had a humorous air about it, so when you are looking to memorize something conjure up a rhyme that will cause you to laugh at how crazy the picture is in your mind.

In another study, researchers found that the method of loci was a great way to retain new information. Those who participated in the study that used the memory technique scored higher on the assessment than the ones who didn't. Method of loci is a memory technique with a lot of potential to use the zaniest parts of your imagination. To master this technique, you visualize a location that you are very familiar with, such as your home, and put the information you need to learn in this location. To improve your recall, you can allow your imagination to run wild. This technique is also referred to as a memory palace, which we will talk about a bit more later on.

Use Your Imagination
It really helps if you can fully immerse yourself in your imagination so that you can improve your memory recall. Researchers at the University of Arizona discovered that people could remember a word better if they were told to think about how well it described them. When you visualize information, picture yourself interacting with the place or object. You can also

engage your senses so that you can imagine how it tastes, smells, and feels.

Not everybody is born having an amazing memory, but everybody is able to use their imagination in order to train their brain to remember more information they have learned. Boris Konrad and Martin Dresler discovered that mnemonic brain training is something everybody can use to improve their memory, not just those special memory champions. The only thing you need is visualization and imagination.

So, if imagination has such a huge impact on memory, imagine what could happen if you make it a part of your daily habit to improve your imagination? I want you to try this simple activity. This will take less than three minutes and is the perfect way to exercise your visualization ability to allow your imagination to run free.

- Pick an object you have around you – we'll go with your cell phone.

- Now, shut your eyes and take about ten seconds or so to describe how your phone looks.

- Open your eyes and then look at your phone to see if there are any other details that you could have described.

- Close your eyes again, and describe everything that you can remember about your phone.

- Once done, open your eyes again and pick a different object – we'll say it's your laptop.

- Now, you are going to engage your imagination. You want to picture your cell phone interacting with your laptop in some way. Allow this to become crazy. Perhaps, your phone could have eyes and arms, and it starts to type out a book on your laptop.

- Shut your eyes one last time and describe a little short story in great detail so that you bring this to life in your mind. Remember, you want it to be bizarre and funny.

This is not only a great way to improve your visualization ability, but it will also allow you to work out your imagination. When you see objects in your mind, and you describe how they interact, you create memorable associations that you won't be able to forget.

If you want, you can start doing this every single day to improve your imagination and visualization. Instead of trying to do the complete exercise every day, which could cause you to become burned out, you can turn it into tiny habits. On the first day, you will just do the first step or so. Over a five day period, you will do more steps until you are doing the complete exercise every day. This will then become automatic.

To make sure that you do this every day, you can pick an anchor that will trigger this action. This could be after you finish your breakfast; you pick an object to describe. Once finished, you celebrate in some way.

Create Pictures

Now that you know and understand the importance of imagination when it comes to remembering things, let's look at the first step in remembering what you want. We are going to create mental snapshots of events. This is a great way to remember events in your life as well.

When you engage your full attention on what is presently happening, it will encourage the creation of stronger, clearer memories of important things. A person's ability to remember detailed events is normally not automatically strong. With the use of mental snapshots, you can have better success in creating long-lasting memories. If you despise your episodic memory, don't worry. Instead, you're going to be able to snap a mental picture or two to improve your odds of remembering things.

Creating photo albums, recording a video of an event, or writing it down in your journal are great ways to preserve memories. But you can't always carry around these physical memory aids. A clear mental image that you can instantly recall is a precious commodity. There are two main types of memory, episodic and semantic. Episodic memory is the memory of events and is one type of declarative memory. Semantic memory is the recollection of general knowledge and concepts.

Your episodic memory is made up of memories of emotions, times, and places associated with a certain event that has happened to you. When you think about your high school graduation or what you ate for breakfast, you are using your episodic memory.

There are some people who are able to recall details easily. There are some people who are so good at this; they have what is known as hyperthymesia, or "excessive remembering." This isn't always a good thing, though.

Jill Price is one of the first hyperthymesic. She can recall every little detail of her life since the age of 14. She finds it distracting, exhausting, uncontrollable, and non-stop.

But this memory trick is for those who are burdened by a perfect memory. This is for those who find themselves saying "I don't remember that." This won't require any special tools. All you need is your brain, an intention, eyes, and a couple of steps that a lot like using a camera.

The important thing to remember when creating a mental snapshot is making sure that you are completely focused on what is happening. You could be there and soaking in most of what is going on, but without realizing it, you aren't connected deeply enough with the special moments. To create a mental snapshot, you have to be able to zoom in on the little things. We will use a wedding as an example of a moment that you want to remember forever.

1. Watch the scene with intent. Make sure you keep your head still. Gaze at what is going on with concentration and focus. Tell yourself that it is important that you are able to

remember the details of what is going on. Carefully observe all of the colors of the scene. Look at the position and arrangement of the wedding party. The dresses that the bridesmaids are wearing. The way the room is lit, how the flowers. Really drink in the moment.

2. Slowly blink your eyes. With your eyes focused intently on what you see before you, you will want to click your brain's camera "shutter" by blinking once at half-speed. Basically, you will want to close and open your eyes at half the speed that they normally move. You can even imagine hearing a "click" like you would when taking a picture.

Now, you will want to take a moment to review the picture you just took in your mind's eye. Close your eyes for a second and conjure up the picture in your memory. Take a mental look at the image you just captured. If you find that your picture is a bit fuzzy, open up your eyes and take a harder look at what you were trying to remember, and then take another snapshot.

This can be used when trying to remember just about anything. It could even be helpful when it comes to remembering a grocery list as well.

Intense focus is what is important to come up with permanent and clear mental snapshots. Focus requires mental effort. The more you practice this technique, the clearer and more detailed your images are going to become.

You shouldn't try to take dozens of pictures like you would with a camera. Instead, you should use your max concentration in just a few moments that represent the entire event. For some things, one mental snapshot could be enough.

Your most lucid memories are likely connected with powerful emotions. Events that you connected to peak moments of loss, fear, accomplishment, and joy are recalled more easily and vividly.

The Rule to Remember Anything
When it comes to memorizing things, there are three steps that you can take that will help you to remember anything and everything. First, you will make sure that you engage as many senses as possible, this means sound, smell, touch, sight, and sometimes taste. Second, you will emphasize your mental image you have created with your senses. This means that you will over exaggerate it so that you couldn't possibly forget it. Lastly, you will make it exciting. This means that you will picture your image doing something. Let's look at each of these steps a bit more.

Use Your Senses

While the mental snapshot technique is helpful in remembering things, there are many other mental image techniques that can help you to remember things. There isn't one best technique; the important thing is that you make it as memorable as possible. This means using as many senses as possible.

Have you ever been walking down the street distracted by your own memories and thoughts, and then you caught a whiff of something? A bakery down the street is making cookies, and the smell of the butter, sugar, and eggs takes you back to another time and place.

Instead of walking down the street, you are in your childhood home playing hide and seek outside while your mother is cooking. Everybody experiences where an image, taste, sound, or smell sends then back in time.

The five senses have the ability to clearly evoke memories of the past and free positive emotions like happiness and pleasure, or it can evoke feelings of anger and fear. A song can make you think of a special moment with an important person, or a road trip you have taken with friends. What's around you can transport you back to the memories of your teens and what you experienced at a certain place.

Of your five senses, the mind may like thinking in pictures, but the sense of smell is the strongest when it comes to evoking memories. A simple scent can unleash a rush of emotions. The smell of perfume, wet grass, or the aroma of coffee can cause you to experience various emotions.

1. Use Smell

When you create a mental image, make sure that you try to use your sense of smell. Smell is most closely connected with your hippocampus, which a brain structure that is responsible for your memory. Smell is also connected with the limbic system, which the emotional area of your brain. All the other senses have to move along a path to reach the areas of the brain that control our emotions and memories.

This is the reason why smell will often awaken vivid memories and bring up sensations that mix sadness and sensitivity, which often called nostalgia. One study performed by Silvia Alava, psychologist, found that people were able to remember 35% of what they smell and around 5% of what they see.

The study explained that when a person smells perfume, it is not only registered in the brain, but it is also associated with an emotion that you are feeling in that moment. When you smell that perfume again, you will experience the emotions again.

2. Use Sight

All of your mental pictures are going to use sight because you can visualize them. As far as sight bringing up memories, a picture of a landscape, bedroom, or object can bring up a moment in your life that you enjoyed. There can also be moments where we feel as if we have experienced a moment before, known as déjà vu.

There are two theories for the experience of déjà vu. One theory explains that when you register an event in your memory, there are parts of the brain that registers things slower than the others, and déjà vu happens when the last parts of the brain process the event. The other theory suggests that sometimes an event create a delay of memories that we have a real or imaginary relationship with the memory.

3. Use Taste

This sense may be a bit hard to use in a memory technique, but if you can figure out how to add in taste, great. When we eat something, the brain will use the sensations of taste with the information that you have stored in your memory, and it will look for data concerning certain things that you can relate with the taste, previous situations, or other types of foods that have had similar stimuli.

4. Use Hearing

Next, you will want to add sound to your mental images. Everybody has, at some point, created a mental soundtrack from songs they have listened to. Our life doesn't come with a spontaneous soundtrack, but a lot of memories will be triggered by a familiar piece of music.

5. Use Touch

Lastly, you want to try to use touch in your mental image as well. Of the five senses, touch is the weakest one. Most of the time, one of your other senses will trigger a memory before you have to use the sense of touch. That said. You can still use touch in your mental picture so that you can be sure that something will trigger your memory.

Create Emphasis

Now that you know that you need to use all of your sense to create a vivid memory, let's look at creating a mental image with emphasis that you won't be able to forget.

To create a strong mental connection with new information, you have to make sure that your images are memorable because it's too easy to forget ordinary things. It's easy to remember the outrageous, the impossible, and the silly. Do you remember what you ate for dinner on Monday three weeks ago?

More than likely not. But, I bet you remember your first day of high school or your first date because these are all memorable events. When it stands out, you are more likely to remember it. That means you need to make sure that your mental images stand out in some way. Here are a few things to remember when it comes to making memorable images:

- Substitute one item with a different item.

- Has the image come alive?

- Exaggerate the amount of something, which means picture a million of whatever you need to remember.

- Exaggerate a proportion of the item. This could mean that the item is huge in your mind, or only a part of it is large, kind of like a caricature.

Maybe you want to remember that the capital of Peru is Lima. Lima sounds like a lemur, so you could picture a giant lemur swinging around on a tree.

Create Action

The last thing you need to do is bring your mental image to life. Think about when you try to remember a phone number. You might find that you move your fingers in order to help you remember the number. The movement helps you remember something, so when you make your mental image move, you will be able to remember it more easily.

Think back to the mental image of the lemur swinging on the trees. The image had movement; it was alive. Now, this can also be even funnier. Let's look at another mental image to remember the capital of a country. For this one, we will use Montevideo. It is the capital of Uruguay. Now, to me, Montevideo sounds like movie video.

To add movement and to make it crazy, we could picture a large VHS tape (remember those?) take their little VHS family to see a new movie. That's an image you are likely not to forget. And, to wrap things up and connect everything, in this image of the VHS tape family going to the movies, we could add in some other senses. You can imagine the smell of the popcorn of a movie theatre and the sticky feel of the movie theatre floor. See how this all comes together to create something you will always remember? I'll bet you won't forget that Uruguay's capital is Montevideo.

Photographic Memory

The next thing we are going to look at is different ways to create a photographic memory. This means that you will be able to remember different things, like names, places, numbers, and words, in great detail. The photographic memory that most people refer to means that people remember things without the use of mnemonic devices. We are going to use mnemonic devices to create a photographic memory of sorts.

People who have amazing skill at memorizing things, like chess players who can best opponents while blindfolded, or card sharks who can memorize the order of a shuffled deck of cards are typically only good at one task. They can memorize the one thing they are good at. You don't want that, do you? You want to be able to memorize anything and everything that you see or hear, right? That's what we are going to learn to do.

Pages, Words, and Lists

Through evolution, the brain has become great at dealing with sensory information. Through correctly interpreting the five senses, the mind is able to understand the environment. Sight has become the most developed of the human senses. This is why the brain has become extremely good at processing and storing images; especially when they are concrete and real-world objects. Trying to remember abstract symbols, like printed words, is inefficient and unnatural. Words are great ways to communicate, but they aren't the best way for our brain to process information.

Imagery, as you know, is the real language of the mind. Images are the vocab of the mind and the building blocks of any language. When I tell you to think about a horse, what is first the thing that comes to mind? Is it the sequence of letters, H-O-R-S-E? Of course not. The first thing you think of is the picture of a horse; you might even be able to tell me what color it is. Aren't dreams always in images? Pictures are how the mind talks to you, and we need to use that.

To complete understanding the effect that images have for memorizing things, let's take a look at your first memorization technique known as memory pegging. This is a fun little technique and is a great way to memorize words and lists. This is based on thinking in pictures, which you will soon realize most memory techniques will require you to do so.

Before we dive into the technique, I'm going to give you a bit of a challenge. I want you to memorize a list of ten items. You can write this down and study them for about two minutes and then put away the list and don't look at it again. Here is the list:

1. Sausage
2. Eggs
3. Beer
4. Tape
5. Chewing gum
6. Milk
7. Stamps
8. Kale
9. Espresso
10. Tomato

Just like when you learn a new language, you will need to learn basic vocabulary first. We're going to start with some useful words: the numbers one through ten. When you bring the numbers to your visual language, you will be able to use the numbers to memorize your list of words.

There are lots of different ways to change the numbers into images. The best way to do this is to use images that resemble the shape of the numbers. When you remove the abstract symbols of the numbers and replace them with a vivid and colorful image, you will get a better mental picture. Here are a few suggestions:

1. Straw
2. Clothes hanger
3. Lips
4. Kite
5. Chair
6. Croquet mallet
7. Hockey stick
8. Snake
9. Tennis racket
10. Bat and a ball

You can use whatever you feel like you will be able to remember more easily. Once you have created your list of images, take a few images to familiarize yourself with them. These are what will become your pegs, and, once you have learned them, you will be able to use them over and over so that you can memorize everything.

Now that you have your initial vocabulary of images, you will be able to memorize new ones by creating associations between them. All you have to do is combine both images and create a new image. Now you have to use your imagination, remember what we talked about earlier? There is one rule when you do this; it has to be outrageous.

You want it to be as nonsensical, animated, extraordinary, unusual, offensive, ridiculous, and crazy. You want to remember these things, right? Think about what we talked about in the last chapter. The crazier, the better. If it is boring, you are doing it wrong.

If we think back to our grocery list, how can we connect sausage with a straw? You could start by picturing yourself trying to eat a piece of sausage by sucking it up through a straw. If you are able to use your other senses, great, and you can add more imagery to the scene. Think about how hard it would be to try and suck a cooked piece of sausage up through a straw and the force at which you would have to suck. That's going to start hurting, right?

Let's do this again with the second item on the list. We have eggs and a clothes hanger. This one will likely get pretty crazy. You could imagine a row of eggs sitting on the clothes hanger or any other crazy picture that you can think of.

I'm sure by now you get the idea. When you first do this, it can seem like a lot of work to go through each item, but it's not. This action will eventually become automatic, and it's fun.

When you have to recall the list, there's really not much you have to do. The recall will be automatic. All you have to do is ask yourself what the first item is. For number one, you see the straw, and immediately, you see yourself trying to suck sausage up through the straw.

Now, I want you to try to write down the grocery list from earlier in the same order without looking at it. Give yourself a point for each correct word and another point if it was in the correct place. How did you do? The majority of people will get 12 out of 20. If they were asked again a week later without knowing they would be, they would get an abysmal five.

When the pegging method is used, the results are mind-blowing. They typically get a perfect 20, and it normally remains consistent when asked a week later. This is true even when they use the method for the first time.

Link and Story

The next methods we are going to look at are the link and story methods. These are great methods when it comes to remembering lists. The link method is one of the easiest memory devices out there. It helps by creating simple associations between items that are on a list, linking them with a vivid image that holds that item.

You then take the first image and create a connection between it and the next item on your list. You could do this by smashing them together in your mind, place one on top of the other, or so on. You continue through your list in the same manner, linking each item to the next.

The story method works much in the same way, linking each item together with some memorable story feature. The way the story flows and the strength of your images will provide you with cues to retrieval the list.

It is possible for a person to remember a list of words through association only, but, it normally works best when you attach the association to a story. Otherwise, if you forget one association, you could end up forgetting the rest of your list.

Given how fluid this device is, it's important that the images you create are as vivid as you can possibly make them. Let's take a look at how you can use the link and story method to remember a list of towns. The list is Belfast, Derry, Lisburn, Strabane, Downpatrick, Greenisland, Bangor, Newry, and Larne.

Using the link method:

This will use a series of images coding the information:

- A BELl (Belfast) rang down at the DAIRY (Derry) farm.
- The DAIRY farm was BURNing (Lisburn) to the ground.
- This caused the STRAy (Strabane) dog to leave is hiding place.
- PATRICK ran DOWN (Downpatrick) to the fire to help the STRAy dog.

- PATRICK says that the only thing left was a GREEN ISLAND (Greenisland).

- The GREEN ISLAND had a few BANGs (Bangor) and dents in it.

- Besides the BANGs, it was good as NEW (Newry).

- The almost NEW island was used in the LAuNdRy (Larne) as a reminder of the dairy.

There doesn't have to be a point or some reason for the sequence of your images. There just needs to be some link between each so that you can remember the next.

Belfast, Derry, Lisburn, Strabane, Downpatrick, Greenisland, Bangor, Newry, and Larne

Using the story method:

Instead of creating a list of images, you could create an image of the list by creating a vivid story.

The worker rang the BELl FAST (Belfast) to get the attention of the DAIRY (Derry) employees to the fire. The building was BURNing (Lisburn) quickly, but the STRAy (Strabane) dog managed to escape. PATRICK ran DOWN (Downpatrick) the hill to see what he could salvage from the fire. The only thing still standing was a GREEN ISLAND (Greenisland). Besides a few BANGs (Bangor) and dents, the island was good as NEW (Newry). Patrick took the island to the local LAuNdRy (Larne) so that it could be used.

Both of these tools are great ways to remember lists of words. The link method is the most basic technique and easy to create, and the story technique is very similar by linking the words together in a single image.

Acronyms

Another way to remember words or lists are through using acronyms. Acronyms are pretty hard to forget once you have a good one in mind. You can come up with your own for a list of items, or you can see if there is one that already exists. Common acronyms for musicians are, "Every Good Boy Does Fine," to remember the lines on the treble clef, and FACE to remember the spaces. Then you have "Good Boys Do Fine Always," for the lines on the bass clef, and "All Cows Eat Grass" for the spaces.

Another common acronym is HOMEs to remember the Great Lakes; Huron, Ontario, Michigan, Erie, and Superior.

Numbers

Have you ever felt the need to recite pi up to the 22,500 decimal digit? Maybe not, but have you ever really wanted to easily remember birthdays, PINs, passwords, phone numbers, and those types of things? Most everybody does. The problem is, our brains aren't always that great at memorizing numbers. The problem with numbers is that they are abstract concepts. While they may be represented visually by symbols, they don't feel all that real or fun for the brain. The brain tends to work better when it is provided with vibrant and lively images. Numbers don't come close in providing us that.

In our society, we are bombarded with new numbers: passcodes, PINs, ZIP codes, debit and credit card numbers, telephone numbers, and so on. Even if all of these numbers are programmed into your smartphone, it's still easier, not to mention, more secure to keep your most frequently used numbers in your mind.

When something doesn't mean something to you, it's quite hard to remember. Think about this for a minute. If you have ever owned a dog or even saw one at some point and I say the word dog, it is going to bring up all of the memories that you have about dogs and you are going to remember that word without difficulty. But when it comes to numbers, the majority of us don't have that kind of attachment to them.

So, if you are interested in remembering numbers, you have to give them meaning. Let's cover some of the best ways to memorize numbers in an easy manner.

- Create Associations

Everybody has a few numbers that are important to them, such as anniversaries, favorite football players, birthdays, or the amount of 10-cent wings you are able to devour at all-you-can-eat night. The secret to being able to remember new numbers is to figure out a connection between the numbers you need to remember and the numbers that you already have memorized.

If you are struggling to find an association for a number, try moving to the next number because this could end up triggering a memory that you will be able to use to link the first number. For example, if you need to memorize the number 1312, but you are struggling to associate 13 with something, you can move onto 12. 12 could make you think of *Cheaper by the Dozen,* and this could trigger the thought of a baker's dozen being 13.

- Make Long Numbers Short

The average person is only able to hold around seven arbitrary units of information at a time in their working memory. But when you chunk items in some fashion, you can improve your recall capacity. This is the main reason why phone numbers are separated into groups of digits instead of one long strand. Try to memorize this strand of numbers: 7986542872. If you try to interpret this as just a strand of 10 separate numbers, you will find this pretty hard to memorize. But if you are able to find two important dates within the sequence, you will only need to recall three chunks, and then remember won't be a problem.

- Try to Find Patterns

When it comes to long number strands, try to find relationships in the numbers. Do the first two numbers add up to equal the third? Do you notice a sequence of even or odd numbers? Then you can use those patterns to come up with a story with the more arbitrary numbers. For example, if you have the number 0123 7900, you can see the pattern of "0123" and then you can figure out how you can use this to remember 7900. For this example, you could come up with something like, once I max out my credit limit of $7900, I am going to have to start over at zero and build it up again a dollar at a time, 1, 2, 3.

- Actively Learn

Our muscles tend to remember things better than the brain, so you should just think the number. Say the number out loud at least three times. When you speak the number out loud, the brain will have to tell your mouth muscles how to say it and then your ears have to hear the words and pass along the information. This will make you have to use quite a few more areas of your brain. Then, you shouldn't stop there. You should then write the numbers down as well, or you could try to sing them to a memorable tune.

- Repeat

After you have memorized the number, set a time and do nothing but think about the number and any of the associations you have created with it. This should be done one hour after you have learned the number. Research has found that one hour after learning something new is the time in which the memory tends to be the most vulnerable to forgetting the information, degrading the information, or misinterpreting it. Then, in 24 hours, repeat the number again. Do this again one week after you have learned it, and then again after a month. The idea of all of this is to repeat the information around the time that you are about to forget the information, in increments of time that expand as time goes by, so that the number is stuck in your long-term memory. Whatever your brain has managed to learn after 30 days is probably going to stick with your.

- Visualize the Shape a Number Makes on a Keypad

There are a lot of people that will use this technique to remember phone numbers, but this is also great for ZIP codes, PINS, and credit card numbers, especially if you tend to learn better visually. This is extremely useful when numbers create an obvious pattern, such us an "L", "X", or a straight line.

- Convert to Images

There are two ways you could do this. You could set out to learn the major memory system, or you could simply assign the numbers 1 through 9 a letter equivalent, such as A equals 1, B equals 2, and so one. So if you have just created a new PIN number to 3647, you could change the numbers to the letters CFDG. You can then think up a sentence that uses those letters, like "Criminal Fiends Don't Get," and this could be fleshed out to, "criminal fiends don't get this number." This is likely something you would have an easier time remembering.

People who are memory competition competitors will take this method a step further and create an image or some action for every single number from 0 to 99. For instance, the number 36 would be a match and the number 47 would be a rock. They would then try to come up with a mental image that blends those two objects together. This is known as the major memory system, and can become quite confusing.

So, let's try to use the different pieces of information to remember a random ZIP code. Let's try 90089. Right off the bat you know that there are two zeros in the center, but that might not mean anything. There aren't any interesting patterns that they make on the keypad. Next we can chunk up the number: 90, 08, 89, 900. None of them stand out to me, so I'll do a quick Google search to see if anything comes up. The number 90 could refer to Nike Total 90, a sports apparel company that supplies soccer equipment. The number 89 could call up the 2017 film *89* that is about a soccer match between Liverpool and Arsenal in 1989. Then all you would need to remember is the extra 0 between the 90 and 89.

The next thing you would need to do is to repeat this after an hour, 24-hours, and then see how well you can remember it a week from when you learned, and so on. According to the experts, the odds are in your favor.

Places

Memorizing places are just as easy as memorizing numbers, maybe more so. The key memorizing everything is creating images that you can't forget. In ancient times, people would use mental images to help them memorize all types of material. These were commonly used for hundreds of years.

We're going to look at how to use a powerful technique to help you memorize the capitals of the US states. This technique can be used to remember any place that you want. This will work differently than our list of towns in Ireland. We aren't listing here. We are creating visualizations and associations.

This should be a fun technique so that you can recall the capitals, or whatever place you choose, with ease. You also want to make sure that you are clear with your images so that you don't end up confusing the city and states.

We know that the brain likes images, just think about how easy it is to picture your home. That means we need to create images just as vivid to help you associate the capital and state. These are going to be new images to you, so you will need to make them memorable. This means that you need to have a lot of fun when it comes to creating these mental images.

The secret to this technique uses actions, places, and objects that represent the sound of the names. This isn't all that tricky. As long as you get fairly close to it, your brain will step in and do the rest. The examples we will look at will show you how to do this. You will then be able to use this trick whenever you need for whatever you need.

1. Atlanta, Georgia

First, we are going to memorize the capital of Georgia, which is Atlanta. We are going to create a mental image so strong that we couldn't possibly think about a different or state. First, let's create a mental image for Atlanta. If you say this slowly, you get the sounds, at-lan-ta. To create a memorable image, maybe it becomes "ant land on." You only need to close to the real thing. A picture for "ant land on" we could picture an ant wearing a parachute having just jumped out of a plane.

Next, we have to think about Georgia. To me, I think of the name George. This could go one of two ways, Curious George or George Washington. For our imagery, we'll go with George Washington. It's very easy to picture George's face on a dollar bill.

Now, we need to link the two images together. We want to make sure that we remember that Atlanta is the capital of Georgia. To do so, think about a one dollar bill with George Washington looking up into the sky with horror as an ant parachute down and lands on his face.

To lock this mental image into place, think about it a few times. It's an odd picture, so it should stick in your mind. We'll look at a couple of more examples to help you get the hang of this trick.

One note, however, is that when you are dealing with states like North and South Caroline or North and South Dakota, you want to make sure you differentiate the states so that you don't get confused. The easiest way to do this is to add a polar bear to the North state because polar bears live near the North Pole. Then add a penguin to the South state because penguins live near the South Pole.

2. Little Rock, Arkansas

The next state and capital we will look at is Little Rock, Arkansas. It's easy to picture a bunch of little rocks raining down from the sky to remember Little Rock. Then we need to break down Arkansas, which is pronounced ark-an-saw. This makes me think of an ark and a saw.

To create a link between the two, picture an ark sailing down the river. It is raining, but instead of raindrops, it's raining little rocks. These rocks hurt, so the sailor is trying to bat them away with a saw.

3. Frankfort, Kentucky

For our last example, we will create a mental image of Frankfort, Kentucky. To me, I would break Frankfort down into the sounds frank fork. For frank, we'll use a hot dog, and for fork, we will think of the metal eating utensil.

The word Kentucky breaks down into the sounds king tuck e. We will get rid of the e and just use king tuck. To bring together the images, we can picture a king holding a giant fork that he uses to tuck hot dogs (franks) down his pantaloons.

As long as you make sure that you practice recalling these images a few times after you come up with them, you shouldn't have a problem remembering them. Now, we could continue and go through every state, but these mental images work best when you come up with them yourself. They become personal to you at that point, and you will be less likely to forget them.

Names

The last thing we are going to look at is how to memorize names. This is something everybody probably wants to know how to do. There's nothing worse than running into a person that you know, but you can't think of their name. According to Psychology Today, this only gets worse with age. Nearly 85% of middle-aged and older adults will forget names.

It's understandable, though. When you meet a person, there is a lot that happens, from the way they look to the conversation and other distractions that take place. Rest assured, we can fix this problem so that you are no longer faced with that awkward moment. The technique we are going to look at is SISA: speak, imagination, specify, another.

1. Speak

First, you speak. This means that you repeat their name. When a person tells you their name, don't just smile and nod and then continue talking. You want to plug the name into your conversation. This can be done like so, "I'm Joseph." "Hi, Joseph, nice to meet you." If that doesn't work for you, can also ask a question using their name, such as "How long have you been working in marketing, Joseph?"

You can use their name throughout the conversation but do so sparingly. There's no need to come off overly salesy or repetitive. When you end the conversation, make sure you use their name again while looking them in the eye. Use this moment to commit it to memory.

2. Imagination

Several experts suggest that you create a mental image when you first hear a person's name. You can also create a verbal game by creating an alliterative sentence about the information you know about the person. For example, if you know they are from Maine and their name is Mary, it could be "Mary from Maine." The same can be done with their job.

To really engage your mind and memory, create a mental image of something that sounds like their name. This can then be combined with something that you know about them. If you met a person named Brock, it sounds like rock. If you knew he lived near their Rocky Mountains, then you could picture him hiking up a large rock.

3. Specify

The next thing to do is look at special features they have. When you notice these things about them, you can use them in your imagery from the last step so that you are certain about the person when you see them. This could even be a scent. Maybe they always wear the same perfume. The first thing that jumps out at you about them is the best feature that you should use in your mental image to help you remember their name.

Maybe they wear the same purple scarf no matter where they go. They could have really bright blue eyes that you can't help but notice. It could be that they have multicolored hair. Anything that you can pick out about that person that you couldn't possibly confuse with another person is exactly what you should add to your image.

4. Another

The last step to remembering a name is to associate their name with another person you already know. Chances are, you will immediately think of the other person you know when the new person introduces their self. This doesn't even have to be a person that you know personally.

Let's say you meet a woman named Carrie. This person is easy for you to associate with because your sister's name is Carrie. Then you meet a person named Charlie. You don't know any Charlie's personally, but you can associate them with the actor Charlie Sheen. The next time you meet either of these people, you will be able to remember their name by picturing the person you already know with them.

While this last tip I'm going to share isn't a part of the SISA technique, it can be helpful for a lot of people. Ask them to spell their name. This is mainly for people who have unusual names. This will help you to create a visual image of their name as they spell it out. If you are in a professional setting, you could ask for their business card instead.

Mind Mapping

Mind mapping was created by Tony Buzan. Mind mapping is a great way to get information into and out of your brain. It is a logical and creative means of taking notes and making notes that will map out ideas.

Every mind map will have certain things in common. They have an organizational structure that goes out from the center and uses images, color, words, symbols, and lines according to brain-friendly, simple concepts. This allows you to convert a monotonously long list into a highly organized, memorable, and colorful diagram that works with your brain's natural ability to do things.

A simple way to understand mind mapping is to compare it to a city map. The center of the city is where the main ideas are located. Main roads lead from this center to show your main thoughts. The secondary roads show your secondary thoughts, etc. Special shapes or images can stand for relevant ideas or interesting information.

The best thing about mind mapping is you can write down your ideas in any order when they enter your mind. You are not constrained by any specific order. Just write down any or all ideas and worry about organizing them later.

This wonderful technique has been used by more than 250 million people throughout the world to help with tasks like communicating information, studying, teaching, managing projects, organizing, finding new opportunities, brainstorming, and a lot more.

Mind maps can be used for all cognitive functions like analysis, creativity, learning, and memory. This process involves a combination of visual-spatial arrangement, color, and imagery. It maps out your thoughts by using keywords that make associations in the brain that sparks more ideas.

There are several software programs out there that will help you organize your thoughts, and it will export them into an easy to read list.

It is possible to mind map with paper and pen but why not use technology and save yourself time. There are many elements to think about like the center image, keywords, colors, images, and branches.

A mind map is an external mirror of your own natural thinking that makes it easier by using powerful graphics. This gives us a key to unlock the unlimited potential of our brains.

There are five main characteristics to mind mapping:

- The main focus, subject, or idea is the central image
- The main themes run from the center image like branches
- These branches will have a main image or word drawn on its lines
- Lesser important topics are on the "twigs" of the branches
- These branches create a connected structure

How to Mind Map

Here are the steps to create a mind map:

1. Figure out a central idea

This is the starting point of your mind map and will represent the main topic you want to explore.

This needs to be in the center of the paper and need to include an image that shows your main topic. This will draw attention to and will trigger further association because our brains will respond better to visual stimulation.

Take time to make the main idea personal. This strengthens the connection you have with the content of the mind map.

2. Add branches

Now you need to get your creative juices going and add in some branches. The main branch that goes from the center image is the main ideas. You can explore each branch in great detail by adding smaller branches.

The best thing about a mind map is that you can constantly add new branches and you aren't restricted to only a few options. The structure will come naturally as you add in more ideas while your brain draws associations from the various concepts.

3. Add keywords

Once you have added a branch to your mind map, you need to add key ideas. One important aspect to mind mapping is putting one word on every branch. Using just one word will spark numerous associations as compared to using a lot of words or phrases.

Let's say you want to throw a surprise party for your boss. You create a branch that says "surprise party." Now you have limited the brainstorm to just aspects of a party. If you only use the word "surprise," you can go out with other words like cake, presents, party, decorations, etc.

Having just one word on each branch works great for chunking information into themes. Using keywords triggers connections if the brain and lets you remember more information.

4. Color the branches

Mind mapping encourages the entire brain to think because it sparks numerous cortical skills like special, creative, numerical, and logical.

Overlapping these skills will make your brain synergetic and keeps it working at its optimal level. When you keep these skill isolated from each other doesn't help the brain develop. This is what the brain was designed to do.

An example of the entire brain thinking is to color code our mind map. Color coding will link the visual and the logical. This allows your brain to make shortcuts. This, in turn, lets you analyze, highlight, identify, and categorize more connections that you might not have thought about before.

Colors make things more engaging and appealing as compared to monochromatic, plain images.

5. Use images

Images can convey more information than an essay, sentence, or a word. They get instantly processed by the brain and act as stimuli to help you recall information. Images are a universal language that can overcome language barriers.

We have been taught from a young age to process images. Before children learn to read in any language, they can see pictures in their minds that get linked to concepts. This is the main reason behind mind mapping.

Increase Reading Speed

Do you want to be able to read a book effortlessly and quickly? Do you want to learn how to speed read without forgetting what you have just read?

Many people think that speed reading is hard to learn, but it is an art that can be learned by using the right tools and exercises. They think you have to learn how to speed read at an early age and it can't be learned when you get older. This isn't true, as many people have learned to speed read at an older age.

It doesn't matter if you are skimming through blog posts, looking through files for work, or browsing a book, you probably do some sort of reading each day. Trying to get through dense textbooks is hard on your eyes, mentally exhausting, and time-consuming.

With some practice, you will be able to read through dozens of pages in just a few minutes.

1. Scan or skim

Scanning or skimming are two techniques that involve looking for the most important parts first. This will get you ready for what is to come. You probably know a little bit about the text, to begin with, so you won't be surprised if you come upon a confusing part.

Remember that while you are scanning or skimming, it works best when you are reading non-fiction books. It can be done with novels, just skim the chapter to find major plot points, key dialogue points, and character development. Next read at a faster pace than normal.

2. Don't subvocalize

This is the most common factor that slows down reading. This is the most critical and hardest habit to break when learning how to speed read. Sometimes we are limited by how long it takes us to pronounce every word on the page. This is the way the majority reads. We "speak" every word in our mind. This will slow down your reading to how fast you speak. This is around 300 words per minute.

When we say a word out loud, it takes a specific amount of time to pronounce the word. Truth is, we don't have to pronounce the words when we read. We can just absorb them.

If you have ever been reading and realized your lips were moving while you read, this is still subvocalization.

This habit is so embedded in our brains that breaking free of this sound completely impossible. A great trick is to choose a word and look at it for a few minutes in complete silence. There is going to be some subvocalization but just look at the words without wanting to pronounce it. A new habit will be for form.

A good tip to defeat this habit is to begin looking at and thinking about words without needing to pronounce them. This part might feel completely weird at first, and that is normal. You just need to worry about looking at the words without wanting to hear how they sound.

With some practice, you will begin to see a difference between speaking the word and just letting it enter your mind. When you can do this, you will have torn down the largest barrier between speed reading and yourself.

Our brains and eyes can process words a lot faster than that. If you can stop the voice in your head, you could double your reading speed.

If you subvocalize, it is hard to learn how to read faster. This is a hard habit to break. The best and easiest way is to become mindful of it to keep yourself distracted. You could use your finger, chew gum, or listen to music.

3. Read phrases instead of words

In order to increase your reading speed, be mindful of what your eyes are doing. Many people can scan about one and a half inch chunk of words. This depends on the type of text and font size which is usually made up of about five words. Instead of reading every single word, move your eyes and jump from chunk to chunk. Use your peripheral vision to speed up at the start and end of every line. Focus on blocks instead of the first and last words.

If you look at every fifth word, this allows you to take in more at a time and will help you stop vocalizing. Just like all things, it is going to take time and training to be able to do this well. Beginning with textbooks would be the best place to start.

Using a pen or your finger to point at every chunk of words helps you learn the right way to move your eyes over the text. It encourages you to stop subvocalizing.

4. Stop re-reading

The largest time sucker for many people is going back and reading paragraphs or sentences that they didn't understand the first time. They think if they didn't completely understand each word the whole book won't make sense.

You will eventually realize that you aren't getting any comprehension when you re-read. The confusing parts will make sense in context, or they aren't needed to be able to enjoy the book.

An untrained person will use back-skipping or subconscious rereading by misplaced fixation and regression or conscious rereading that makes up about 30 percent of their total reading time. That is a lot of time. Stop having to completely comprehend each thing that is going on or being said. You will quit wasting time reading things you have already read.

5. Read more

Reading is just like all worthy pursuits; it is a skill that will take time to develop. The more you practice, the better you get. Many people think that setting goals are silly. Reading isn't a race. Setting goals will force you to create more time to read. The more you read, the faster you will get.

Remember the best way to enjoy books is to read them at your own pace. Books are meant to be savored. Who cares if you spend countless hours enjoying a great story? There will always be books in the world, and only so much time. I would be better to enjoy the books you want to than to breeze through ones you don't care about.

6. Preview the text

Looking at a film's trailer before you watch the movie will give you some context and allows you to know what you should expect. The same holds true for previewing text before reading it. It will prepare you to get an understanding of what you will be reading. In order to preview text, scan it from start to finish. Pay attention to bullet points, large or bold font, subheadings, and headings. To understand it better, skim through the introductory paragraphs and conclusions. Try to find transitions sentences and look at graphs or images. See how the author structured the text.

7. Have an attack plan

Approaching the text strategically will make a difference in how effectively you will understand the material. The first thing to do is think about what your goals are. What is it you want to learn from this material? Write down some questions you would like to have answered at the end. Figure out what the author's goals were when they wrote the material. Their goal might be describing the whole history of Ancient Greece. Your goal might be just to answer a question about a woman's role in politics. If your goal is more inclusive than the author's, try to find and only read the sections you need.

Change up your attack plan by the kind of material you are reading. If you need to read a science textbook or a large legal file, you will need to read specific passages slower and more carefully than you would read a magazine.

8. Be mindful

In order to read fast and be able to comprehend what you have read takes concentration and focus. Get rid of interruptions, distractions, and external noises. If you realize you are thinking about what you are going to eat instead of focusing on what you are reading, bring your mind back to the material gently. Most readers will read some sentences without actually focusing, then they waste time reading it again to make sure they understand it. If you attentively and carefully approach your reading, you will realize if you don't understand something and this will save you time.

9. Don't read each section

It is a total myth that you have to read each section of text. If you aren't reading something that is important, skip sections that aren't relevant to your purpose. Selective reading makes it possible for you to find the main ideas in most texts.

10. Do a summary

You aren't finished when you have read the last word in a book. Once you have finished reading, write some sentences to summarize what you have just read. Answer the questions you wrote before you began reading. Did you find everything you wanted to find? When you take some time after you have finished reading to write down what you learned, to think, and to gather the information, you will make the material more solid in your mind so you can have better recall. If you are a verbal or visual learner, create a mind map to tell another person what you have learned.

11. Do some timed runs

You have to strategically approach the text, read it actively, and summarize it. All of this takes practice. If you would love to improve your reading speed, time to see how many pages or words you can read per minute. Once you are able to read faster, check in to see if you are happy with how well you are comprehending things.

12. Figure out your baseline

In order to get faster as speed reading, you have to be able to recognize your growth. Before you can measure this, you have to have a baseline. Once you have your baseline, you have to measure your reading periodically and compare it to this baseline.

A good resource to track your results is ReadingSoft.com. This provides you with a consistent, rapid measurement of how fast you are reading. When you take tests regularly, it will be easier to recognize your growth, and this will give you all the motivation you will need to continue.

The main problem with understanding your baseline is it is hard to translate into normal terms when talking about reading a specific amount of words per minute. It is a practical place to start, but it is more important to know how long it takes you to read a page.

If a normal person takes five to ten minutes to read a page, speed readers only need more than two to three minutes. This means that a 200-page book could be read in 400 minutes by a speed reader where a normal reader will take between 1000 to 2000 minutes.

This means a normal reader will spend an extra 13 or so hours on the book. That is more than one half of a day that has been lost.

It isn't easy jumping from reading for 17 hours to being a speed reader. There will be some obstacles in your way, but many of them can be dealt with easily.

13. Use pointers

Using your finger as a guide while reading is usually reserved for children, most people stop doing it once they have learned to read. This trick is handy when learning to speed read.

The largest hurdle in learning to speed read isn't learning the skill but in getting rid of old habits that stop us. One of these habits is reading without a guide. When learning to speed read, a guide is a necessity. This one isn't negotiable.

When you use a guide, your main goal is moving the guide at a constant pace. You should never stop or slow down your finger. It needs to slide from side to side at a uniform speed. By doing this, you will notice if you get stuck or lose any momentum. This is easier than trying to follow along and moving your eyes as quickly as possible.

When you try to move your eyes quickly, you will not be able to maintain a fluid motion because you will eventually hit an obstacle. This will cause you to backtrack, and this causes confusion.

If you have to do this twice on one page, this will add 30 seconds per page. That adds up to an hour and a half that is lost to backtracking on the whole book. You have to learn to think about speed reading as a marathon instead of a race.

Pointers aren't limited to just your finger. You could use a pen, marker, ruler, whatever is handy for you.

14. Don't read unimportant, small words

To understand the way speed readers get fast is to understand that not all words are created equal. There are a lot of small words that don't help you but try to force you to read them. This will only hurt you in the long run.

If you look back at the above point that adding an extra 30 seconds per page could translate to a whole hour and a half think about what could be done when you get rid of all the "to," "is," "the," "if," and other small words. This concept will save you time, but it is yet another skill you need to develop.

The best part of skipping small words is they don't contribute any useful information. This means that skipping them won't ruin your reading experience. Cool, right?

When you skip words, you will get more done. To train yourself to skip the small words, it is simply realizing that you don't need to pay any attention to them. Just let your eyes move across them.

With time, your brain will learn to skip them, and you will be able to scan sentences while skipping insignificant words.

Alternatives to Speed Reading

Reading might not be something you enjoy doing, but you do enjoy books. What do you do now? There are alternatives to you actually reading books.

Many books available to the public can also be found as an audiobook. This allows you to "read" a book while walking, jogging, working, doing laundry, or whatever needs to be done during your day. Some platforms even give you a free trial period to start.

You might have been in a bookstore and found a book that looked very interesting, but the book was just too thick to even think about reading, so you put it back. Days later you are still wondering about that book. What do you do?

There is an app for that. It is called Blinkist. The Blinkist team reads books, finds the main points, and explains them in an easy 15-minute summary. It is basically a web version to the small paperback CliffNotes that most high school students would use to help them on book reports.

Maintaining Memory

You might have taken a class on something to help you in your job. Maybe it was a book about your field of expertise. You might have taken the latest computer course and learned how to use a new system. Within a few weeks or months, you have forgotten everything.

If we don't apply the new knowledge, it is very easy to forget what you learned. Maybe you take notes like crazy while in class. Do you ever get those notes out after the course is over to read back over what you learned? If not, this is the main reason we forget what we have learned.

Everything in this book will help you with your memory so it is extremely important to read this book many times so you get everything you can out of it.

Review
Let's look at how beneficial it is to review information while we explore strategies that will also help.

When learning new information, it is remembered best right after we learn it. We will forget the details as time goes by. Within just a few days, we are only able to recall just a bit of what we had learned.

In order to remember things for a long time, we have to move the information out of our short-term memory into our long-term memory. Short-term memory is the things we currently think about.

To help us do this, we have to review everything we learn and do it often. It will take time to move this information into long-term memory but reviewing it over and over again will help us do it.

These strategies can be used in everyday business situations while helping you improve your memory - things like your client list, details about your client, or recalling information for a presentation.

Reviewing Effectively

Let's look at some strategies that are useful to help you remember information in the long run.

1. Immediately review

Take a few minutes and look over the material right after you learned it. This will help you know that you understand the material. It will reduce the time you need to relearn parts of it when you need it in the future.

While you are reading over the material again, use effective strategies to be sure you are reading intelligently and efficiently. For example, if you have finished reading a chapter in a book, you might only need to look at certain headings and the chapter conclusion to begin putting information into your long-term memory.

2. Rewrite things

Reorganizing and rewriting your notes is a great way to look over information.

This may sound like a waste of time, but rewriting can be an efficient method to reinforce what you are learning. Research has shown that rewriting notes will help clarify what we understand.

An easy way to do this is to put the information we learn into mind maps. These are great for rewriting notes since they force us to make connections between themes and concepts.

You could write down the main points into bullet style or just tidy up your original notes.

3. Schedule time to review

It takes a repeat effort to move information into long-term memory. This is why you need to review information many times.

It is best to do a review one day after the class, then again in a week, a month, and then review the notes a few months from here on out.

Be sure you schedule the time for reviews, or they will get pushed to the side when an urgent matter comes up. Put these reviews on a to-do list or daily planner.

You will find it useful to rewrite your notes during these reviews. Try to jot down what you remember about the class, and compare this to the original notes. This will pinpoint any information that you might have forgotten plus it will refresh your memory.

Getting enough sleep will help your memory, too. Research has shown that we can remember more if we get plenty of sleep. Read on to learn more.

Naps

Researchers have known for a long time that sleep helps memory. Poor sleep has been linked to problems with memory. Researchers have also found that sleeping right after you have learned new things could improve memory retention. If you want a quick memory boost, you should try taking a power nap.

Power Naps Improve Retention

Researchers at Saarland University looked at how an hour long nap helped memory recall in 41 volunteers. These people were asked to learn individual words along with pairs of words. At the end of this learning time, the volunteers were given a test to see what they remembered. The next part of the experiment asked half of the volunteers to watch a movie while the others were allowed to take a nap.

The volunteers were given another test to see how many individual words and pairs of words they remembered. The volunteers who were allowed to take a power nap remembered more words than the ones who watched a movie.

A nap that is between 45 minutes to one hour will improve how well a person can retrieve memory.

Researchers noted the volunteers who took the power nap didn't do any better on the test after the nap. They scored the same on both tests. The volunteers who watched the movie scored a lot worse after watching the movie. Researchers stated that memory after a nap is almost the same as memory after learning a new skill. Power naps should be confused with "microsleep" which could be dangerous.

Look Inside Our Brain

The researchers didn't just look at how well people performed on tests. They wanted to figure out what was happening inside the brain especially what the hippocampus was doing. The hippocampus plays a crucial role in consolidating and transferring the information into long-term memory. Researchers used EEGs to look at "sleep spindles." They thought that if something was strong in memory, the more "sleep spindles" will show up on an EEG.

To minimize the probability that words could be recalled from the prior association, researchers gave the volunteers 90 individual words with 120 meaningless pairs of words. Instead of pairing up the words that that would have any logical association like "peanut – butter" or "table – lamp," they used combinations that didn't have any relation to one another like "juice – carpet."

Using familiarity isn't useful here when trying to remember word pairs since they hadn't ever heard these combinations of words before. They had to access specific memories from their hippocampus.

What exactly does this mean for anybody who would like to improve their memory? Short naps in school or at the office might be enough to improve their learning. When people are in an environment to learn, they need to think a lot about the wonderful effects of sleep.

When you have an important exam looming ahead, think about taking a quick nap right before the test.

Meditation

Having problems with memory happens to everyone as we get older. No one is immune to this problem. There is good news. Meditation has been proven to be a natural solution to help bother short- and long-term memory. Here are some reasons why:

1. Mind strength training

When we begin to age, our mental capacity will peak and then start to decline. When you use your mind to reach higher levels of focus and concentration is essential to meditation. If you can learn to do this, you will be exercising and strengthening your mind. This will help keep it in great shape. When meditating, we are working our mental muscles and thus prolonging our brain's life. This will keep us from suffering from memory loss.

2. Meditation can slow down the process of aging

Stress is a huge factor in the characteristics of aging like memory loss. It can be reduced significantly after starting a meditation program. Most scientists and doctors think that meditation to be the "fountain of youth" for our brains and bodies.

3. Meditation taps into our memory stores

Meditation could help you remember things that you might have forgotten years ago. Since the brain doesn't discard memories, these memories remain stored in our brains subconsciously. We just need to access them.

The tools we need to access our memories are the thing that we lose. Meditation is the best way to harness the subconscious mind. This lets us retrieve information that we thought was completely gone. Meditation allows this to happen naturally and normally.

4. Meditation will stimulate regions of the brain associated with memory

While you meditate, the frontal lobe and hippocampus which are the storage centers for short- and long-term memories, will light up.

This means you are flexing your memory muscle while you are meditation. You information storage centers will multiply and makes sure your brain keeps the ability to store new memories.

5. Meditation will increase focus

We are going to have memory problems from time to time. This comes from not paying attention to specific subjects like names of people you meet. When we can use mindfulness and learn to live in the moment, we will have more recall. Meditation teaches us to do this. We will be able to remember more details since we have actively stored them away as memories and give them significance.

If you would like to give your memory a boost, meditation is the best, most tested, product out there. The benefits of meditation go way beyond our brains.

Turning Procrastination into Productivity

People who like procrastinating will put things off for days even if they know it should have been done two days ago.

What Procrastination Looks Like

Everyone puts off working on things we don't like to do every now and then. Nobody likes making phone calls that are just going to stress us out. Who has ever heard of someone who likes washing the windows, taking out the garbage, or washing the car? Most people will do these things occasionally. People who procrastinate will do this all the time. This is when the problems begin.

Stress Factor

Procrastination can lead to stress. Procrastination makes wishes and plans fail when we should be feeling fulfillment. Vacation packages and theatre tickets sell out before procrastinators can reserve them. Jobs get taken by other people, deadlines go past, and planes leave without them.

Negative Effects

A Procrastination Research Group in Canada at Carleton University created an online survey. They asked a question: "To what extent is procrastination having a negative impact on your happiness?" They received 2700 responses. Around 56 percent replied with "very much" or "quite a bit." About 18 percent replied with "extreme negative effect."

Threatens Happiness

Most of the time procrastination gets trivialized. People who procrastinate will suffer if they fail to reach their goals or their careers crash. In the long run, procrastination can become more than a threat to productivity, happiness, and health: it could carry this threat into our surroundings like community and companies.

Traits

How can you recognize a procrastinator? They will avoid telling the truth about their abilities. They might prefer to have service jobs. They will focus on the past and don't act on intentions. They will make poor estimates on their time. These characteristics are linked to anxiety, depression, self-confidence, self-control, self-deception, non-competitiveness, perfectionism, and low self-esteem.

No Easy Answers

There aren't any easy answers. It isn't about managing time. When you tell a person who procrastinates to "just do it" is similar to telling someone who is depressed to "just cheer up." We have to look at the way people procrastinate to know why they do it and figure out how to fix it.

Why We Procrastinate?

There are many reasons why people procrastinate. Some people who procrastinate usually had authoritarian fathers. People who procrastinate use it as a way to rebel their demands.

Other people put the blame on parents who didn't allow their children room to create their imagination.

Other people think that procrastinators act and think along the lines of "wishes and dreams" while other people get on with their obligations. People who procrastinate will have disorganized thoughts. This means they will be forgetful and don't plan things very well.

How We Procrastinate

Research in the field of procrastination is relatively new, but scientists are beginning to describe different ways to procrastinate. Two common types are decisional and behavioral procrastination.

Decisional Procrastination

This strategy puts off making decisions if you are dealing with choices or conflicts. People that practice high levels of decisional procrastination are afraid of making mistakes and are usually perfectionists. These people seek more information about things before trying to make decisions if they are even able to make a decision at all.

If a procrastinator is over informed, they are in danger of falling prey to self-sabotage called optional paralysis. They make countless choices and feel unable to pick the right one because they are afraid of picking an option that isn't perfect.

Behavioral Procrastination

This is a self-sabotage strategy that lets people shift blame to avoid action. A student might make a bad grade on a test and use an excuse of procrastination. They would rather create an illusion of lack of effort instead of ability. They will then blame any failure on not having enough time.

Procrastinators usually have self-doubt and low self-esteem. They also worry about how people judge how they do things. People who procrastinate look at their self-worth by looking at their abilities. According to this logic, if you don't finish a task, your ability can't ever be judged.

Failure to adequately perform and prolonged procrastination makes a cycle of behavior that will defeat one's self. This will result in a downward spiral of their self-esteem. Self-inflicted shame and degradation like this will translate into mental health problems and stress at some time.

Steps for Change

The very first step to change is insight. The second step is understanding. Once that has been taken care of, then taking a course on behavior modification therapy might help if your procrastination is causing problems in your relationship or work. There isn't a bandage solution for procrastination, anything that will help you take firm steps will help to rebuild healthy levels of self-esteem and achievement along with helping you feel good about yourself.

Purpose

Why in the world do we treat ourselves this way? The solution seems very simple: "just do it". The reality is a lot more complicated, and what makes it worse is procrastination is written in our DNA. Procrastination runs in the family. It is linked with impulsivity and creates a catch-all that regulates our behaviors. Above all that, research says that procrastination is a trait that will be with you for life.

So, what about people who procrastinate? Are they all doomed to a life of absently watching music videos on YouTube?

Great news, no we aren't doomed. Just like people who are inhibited, they can learn to loosen up. People who are worriers can learn to let it go. People who procrastinate can find ways to help them resist impulses and focus.

There are many faces of procrastination. It might simply be choosing pleasure over a discipline. It might be hard to avoid things that are negative. Sometimes we get paralyzed by expectations that become overwhelming. Not to worry, here are some reasons why we procrastinate and a way to overcome each one:

1. Not an urgent task

It might be a deadline for the end of the week, a ringing phone, a crying baby, whatever it is we will pay attention to the thing that is in front of you.

It is hard to prioritize things when they aren't urgent. From saving for retirement to getting the basement organized, everyone has things that they will never do. Because of this, small and large tasks will sit on the bottom of the to-do list for months and maybe years being neglected.

- Solution: Look at the bigger picture

This tendency is annoying but has some significance in evolution. People have been wired to think about present needs stronger than what we might need in the future. This phenomenon is called temporal discounting. On our face is the present, and we pay it more attention.

This remedy takes a broader perspective instead of being nit-picky about the details. Look at daily tasks as if looking at a bigger picture.

If you want to go back to school, but just can't find the time to do it, you take a few steps back. Would this change your life? What are your goals about education? What is your big picture? Looking at a new perspective can help you take action.

When you have decided it is time to take action, now you are faced with a new type of procrastination:

2. Not knowing how to begin or what might come next

We often find ourselves procrastinating because we don't know what to do. We feel disorganized, confused, or overwhelmed. We won't begin since we don't understand what the first step should be.

This type of procrastination isn't just avoiding the task. It is avoiding a negative emotion. Nobody likes to feel clueless or incompetent; this is why we turn to Netflix instead of cleaning the bathroom. We put off what we should do now by doing other things that are more interested. This is called productive procrastination. Anybody who has tried to organize their desk or does shopping online instead of doing their reports will understand this. When we find that perfect outfit before our date makes us feel like we are ready to go.

- Solution: Create confusion

The main point is knowing it is completely normal to feel stupid when beginning a task that you haven't done before.

Create some confusion into the task at hand. Turn the first step into "figuring out the steps". If screaming into a pillow will get you started, them make that step number one.

Others might need another person to help them think. Brainstorm with a friend or coworker to figure out where you should begin.

It is perfectly normal for the start of the task to include messes, do-overs, and turnarounds. It will only feel bad if you make it feel bad.

3. Afraid of failing

Having a bit of perfectionism is bad. Having high standards will lead to high-quality work. Beyonce, Serena Williams, and Bruno Mars all claim to be perfectionists. At time having high standards will backfire. We will blow off projects because we have convinced ourselves that there is no way we can make the standards we have set.

- Solution: Untangle self-worth and performance

Procrastination and perfectionism are linked together. It isn't the high standards that hold you back but the high standards that get mixed with you believing you performance is connected to your self-worth. This combination can stop you in your tracks.

Remember the critical difference between you and the things you achieve. There is a lot more to you than what you accomplish. Just think about your knowledge, taste, politics, friends, travels, experiences, passions, family, identity, the way you treat others, and the challenges you have overcome.

4. We work better under pressure

Most of us know or might have been that child in high school or college who opens up their textbook just before a final exam and still manage to do better than others who have studied all semester.

- Solution: know yourself

Those children were planning ahead in their own way. There are two kinds of procrastination: active and passive. Active procrastination contains strategy. For people who work well under pressure and like the adrenaline rush and focus that comes with having deadlines and they choose to start very close to that deadline.

Passive procrastination is what most people think about when they hear the word procrastination. They get distracted by videos of bicycle riding dogs or squirrels surfing.

It seems like the choice will pay off, too. Passive procrastination can negatively affect a person's GPA, but an active procrastinator's grades will be just fine. We need to know ourselves. If you are a night owl and thrive in that environment, put on a pot of coffee and open that book at midnight.

5. We don't want to do it

What we should do is boring, hard, it's almost quitting time, it's Friday, and we don't want to be here.

There are things that nobody wants to do like getting out of the recliner and going to bed, calling tech support, and taxes. What are you going to do?

- Solution: Compensate and measure

Many college students who loved to procrastinate did it just because there were other more fun alternatives. To their own selves, they aren't blowing off work; they had all intentions of studying but just not now.

These procrastinators know themselves as well as active procrastinators do. They compensated their procrastination by intending to study earlier and more than other non-procrastinators. Basically, they set time aside from the beginning. Guess what? They studied more than the non-procrastinators not a lot but more.

If you would like to stop procrastinating, see the big picture. Understand it is fine to be confused and dazed at the start. Remember you are worthy and always go beyond your achievements. You have to know yourself. Work with your procrastination just as it is and not how you want it to be.

Goals

Many say that humans are geared toward setting and achieving goals. Goals are a part of everyone's life. What you do in your spare time, the things you want to achieve at work, how you behave in your relationships. All things come down to priorities and the things you want to accomplish in all aspects. It doesn't matter if it is a conscious or subconscious choice.

If you don't set objectives or goals, life will become chaotic happening that is out of your control. You are just coincidence's plaything. Accomplishments such as putting a person on the moon, inventing the computer, etc. are the results of goals that were set at some point in time. It was somebody's vision that was recorded and realized.

Why Set SMART Goals?

Setting SMART goals will bring you structure and makes it easier to track your goals. You won't have vague resolutions; SMART goals will create verifiable goals that take you toward your objective along with clear milestones and an estimate of how attainable the goal is. Each objective can be turned into a SMART goal and can bring you closer to your reality.

Setting SMART goals is the best effective but least used tools to achieve goals. When you have created the outline for your goals, it is time to set intermediary goals. By using a SMART checklist, you will be able to evaluate your objectives. Setting SMART goals will create transparency. It will clarify the way the goal came into existence.

What Does SMART Mean?

Try to think of a goal you would like to set right now whether it be professional or personal. In order for your goal to be a SMART one, it needs the following criteria:

Specific

What is it you want to achieve? If you can be very specific in your description, you will have a better chance of getting it. Setting a SMART goal will clarify the difference in saying "I want to have a lot of money" and saying "I want to make $50,000 each month for ten years by creating the next video game craze."

Questions you should ask while setting your goals:

- Exactly what is it I would like to achieve?
- When?
- With whom?
- Where?
- Are there any limitations or conditions?
- How?
- Why do I want this goal?
- Are there any alternatives in attaining this goal?

Measurable

A measurable goal means you have identified exactly what you want to feel, hear, and see when you have reached your goal. This means breaking down the goal into elements that can be measured. You have to have concrete evidence. Being happy isn't evidence. Quitting smoking because you want a healthier lifestyle is.

Goals that are measurable will go a long way to define exactly what you want. Being able to define the physical manifestations of the goal will make it clearer and therefore easier to reach.

Attainable

Can you attain your goal? This means you need to investigate to see if the goal is totally acceptable to you. You need to weigh the costs, time, and effort against the profits or other obligation you have in your life.

If you don't have the talent, money, or time to reach your goal, you will be miserable and fail. This isn't saying that you can't make something that seems to be impossible and make it possible but planning and doing it.

There isn't anything wrong with shooting for the stars.

Relevant

Is the goal relevant to you? Do you really want to run your own company, be the next breakout artist, have a husband and family? You have to decide if you have the guts to do it.

If you don't have specific skills, you can take classes. If you don't have specific resources, you can find them on the internet.

The big questions are: "Why do I want to reach this goal?" "What is my objective behind this goal?" "Will this goal actually achieve that?"

You could have a larger team to make you perform better, but will it actually?

Timely

We've all heard the old expression: "Time is money." Make a plan of everything you do. Everyone knows a deadline will cause people to jump into action. Make deadlines for yourself and go after them. Keep them flexible and realistic. This will keep your morale high. If you are too rigid on time, it could harm the outcome instead of helping you achieve your goals. This isn't how you want to achieve your goals.

One other thing that is important when creating SMART goals is creating it positively. Remember when you focus on something it will increase. If you focus on NOT doing something, you will only think about that one thing. And it increases. Try to achieve daily discipline.

Time Limits
Never think about breaks as a specific number during the day like five or 12. The main question is how long you should work before you take a break.

75 to 90 Minutes

It has been suggested that you take a break after working for 75 to 90 minutes. This is the amount of time where you will be able to concentrate and get work done. This is the length of time most college classes are held. Most professional musicians will practice for this time limit, too.

Working for 75 to 90 minutes will take advantage of our brain's modes: consolidation and focusing. If people work and then take a 15-minute break, it helps their brain consolidate and retain information better.

This works by breaking a pattern, which is called pulse and pause. It expends energy and then renews it. Research has shown that humans will move from full energy and complete focus to mental and physical fatigue every 90 minutes.

When we pay attention to our bodies, we would realize our bodies are sending signals for us to rest and renew. We override these signals with sugar, energy drinks, and coffee. Some might tap into their reserves until they are completely depleted.

52 Minutes

There might be times when you don't have to work for an hour and a half. The good news is you can work for shorter periods of time and still get the benefits of taking a break. Workers who are more productive take regular breaks. They work for 52 minutes and take 17-minute breaks. These employees achieved more tasks without having to work longer. Having regular breaks caused them to be more efficient.

The reason productive employees can get more done in shorter time periods is that they are well rested during working time. They work with purpose during their 52 minutes.

25 Minutes

The Pomodoro Technique is another option. It breaks up extended focus time into short work periods. This technique works for 25 minutes and then takes a break for five minutes. This technique was developed by Francesco Cirillo. He named it after the kitchen timer that was shaped like a tomato he used. This technique works best when one task needs your complete focus.

Finding the correct amount of time for your breaks will take some trial and error. The point isn't the length of the work or break time. It is finding out what cycle works for you. A person's cognitive capacity will decline during the day. You have to create mental breaks to recharge yourself and maintain productivity.

Using the Break

All breaks aren't created equal. People will pick a break time that doesn't always work for their benefit. The popular breaks such as venting about a problem, drinking a cup of coffee, or eating a snack can cause more fatigue.

Many people will choose these things as ways to cope with fatigue, but these breaks don't renew energy. In order to make a break work for you, you have to be able to mentally disengage from work. Morning breaks might include meditation, helping a friend, or talking to a coworker. Afternoon breaks are the most important and need specific activities. The body's energy will go down throughout the day and breaks could reenergize you.

Do some sort of exercise. Regular exercise can increase our energy level and improves metabolism. Most people think that including exercise into a work day is too much. This is why doing longer breaks is very effective. Simple exercises might include a bike ride in the park or walking for 20 minutes.

Naps are a popular afternoon break. Short naps can be invigorating. Many people worry they will fall asleep and sleep longer than they should. There is a very simple solution. It is a little thing called an alarm clock.

Taking a break might like you are slacking off, they are very important to your productivity. It isn't the time you spend working. It is what you get accomplished during that time. Get rid of time as a way to measure success. You can get more done when you take breaks to energize yourself.

Interesting Facts

Foods

If you are worried about memory loss, you could find help in your kitchen. Here is a list of foods that you could add to your diet that have been proven to help with mental clarity.

- Green tea: You might have heard about the antioxidant power of green tea. It can also help boost your memory, too.

- Blueberries: Berries have an antioxidant pigment called anthocyanin that can increase a person's ability to remember. One study that was done over a three-month period showed an improved recall in older adults that drank blueberry juice.

- Extra-virgin olive oil: This oil contains hydroxytyrosol that can increase messages going to the brain and helps with memory.

- Dark chocolate: Any dark chocolate that is at least 70 percent cocoa has flavanols that increase the blood flow to the brain.

- Almonds: These are excellent brain food since they contain proteins that can boost the production of the nerve chemical that can enhance memory

Coffee and Gum

If you have been looking for something to help your memory, look no further than your coffee cup. There is a theory that caffeine can help to improve your cognitive function. Coffee can also lower your risk of developing Alzheimer's disease if drunk during midlife.

If you aren't a coffee drinker, you can try the "pretend coffee" drinks such as chocolate cream, mocha, vanilla, and Swiss to help improve your memory. If you love your daily coffee, this is another reason to continue with your morning cup or two.

What Research is Saying

Recent studies have shown that coffee can improve memory. The study involved 160 volunteers. They were shown various pictures and objects and were told to identify them as either outdoor or indoor items.

After five minutes have passed, they were either given a placebo or a 200mg caffeine pill. They waited 24 hours and were shown the exact same pictures along with some different ones. They were asked to tell whether the pictures were "similar," "old," or "new."

Researchers noted that both groups could accurately tell if the pictures were new or old. The volunteers who were given the caffeine pill had a better memory than the ones who took the placebo. Giving the pill after showing the pictures demonstrated that caffeine improved the volunteer's memories instead of other probabilities like the improvement in focus or concentration.

They did other experiments with 300 and 100 mg doses of caffeine. The performance was better with the 200 mg doses when compared with the 100 mg dose. There wasn't any improvement with the 300 mg of caffeine when compared to the 200 mg doses.

What they concluded was that a dose of 200 mg of caffeine-enhanced memory better than any other does.

They also found that memory wasn't improved if the volunteers were given caffeine one hour before the identification test.

There are many ways that caffeine might help long-term memory. It might block a molecule called adenosine and keep it from stopping norepinephrine. This hormone can have good effects on memory. Further research is being done to understand the mechanisms of how caffeine affects memory.

When older adults drink coffee, they showed improved working memory when compared to others who don't drink coffee.

Another study found that bees who drank coffee remembered floral scents when compared to bees who drank sucrose. The main question with this study is if this can actually translate to humans.

When combining coffee with sugar, research showed that a person's concentration or attention, verbal memory, and reaction time all improved when compared to others who only received sugar or caffeine along with others who took a placebo.

Coffee can also improve spatial memory. Studies have been done that compared normal coffee drinkers with people who don't drink coffee. When both groups drank coffee, their spatial memory improved greatly. What was more interesting was the people who normally drank coffee didn't receive as many benefits from the coffee as the ones who didn't drink coffee.

Just From Coffee?

A study involving women over 65 who had been diagnosed with cardiovascular disease measured how much coffee they drank and then had them do cognitive assessments regularly over a five-year time span. Results showed women who drank more coffee, did better on cognitive tests.

Energy Drinks

What about young people who drink energy drinks? Energy drinks do contain a lot of caffeine but will it also improve cognitive functions. It will increase alertness but doesn't show any difference in cognitive functions when compared to people who were given a placebo.

Caffeinated Gum?

If you would like another way to get caffeine, instead of drinking coffee, you could chew caffeinated herbal gum. This gum can improve memory just like coffee.

Can Coffee Help Extrovert's Memory?

Are you extroverted? One study shows that working memory can be improved by extroverted adults who drank coffee. Another study tried to replicate its findings. This study found that memory and serial recall in extroverted adults improved when they drank coffee. Coffee also improved their reaction speed and how well they received new information.

Potential Benefits

The average American will consume around 300 mg of caffeine each day. They usually get if from soft drinks, tea, and coffee. Many studies say the caffeine can give health benefits. Coffee could reduce developing liver disease. Other studies say drinking between two and four cups of coffee could reduce the thoughts of suicide.

Cautions

There is some bad news that the stimulant in coffee could disrupt sleep even hours after drinking it. Other studies have shown that caffeine from energy drinks could alter how the heart functions properly.

There has been a lot of research done about coffee and how it can affect cognitive abilities and memory. Results can vary, but there is a general idea that coffee can boost cognitive functions. Some studies say that the way you get caffeine is important since coffee works better than other sources.

Just a word of caution in case you decide to drink cup after cup of coffee. There might be health risks for some people. Even small amounts of caffeine could be detrimental to health.

Gum

Students will try any trick to help them through school. It might be munching on snacks or using mnemonic devices. There are lots of various foods that can help with your memory but can chewing gum help? Many studies have been done on the effects of chewing gum and memory, specifically auditory and visual memory.

Chewing gum causes "mastication-induced arousal." No, it doesn't sound pretty, but it does mean what it sounds like. The repetitive motion when chewing gum increases your blood pressure and gives your cells lots of oxygen. This will help you improve your memory and concentrate better.

Just smelling gum can give your memory a jumpstart. You might have wondered why a specific smell can bring up certain memories. The olfactory bypasses the thalamus. This is the main part that processes sensory information. Signals from the olfactory have a pass directly to the amygdala and hippocampus. These parts are linked to memory and emotions.

People who chew gum while learning could recall and retrieve the information faster than people who don't chew gum. This is all thanks to context-dependent effects. This happens because the brain creates a link with chewing gum and learning and creates a habit. Try to chew gum the next time you have a lecture pop a piece of gum in your mouth. When you have an exam, try chewing gum about ten minutes before to boost your recall. You might be pleasantly surprised at how many answers you know.

Chewing gum can also boost cortisol levels and improve your mood. This, in turn, will increase alertness. When you are alert, you will have a better memory.

Mint smells can specifically enhance memory and cognition by lowering stress, clearing congestion, and increases blood flow. Next time you are standing in line at the store, grab some mint gum. You might begin surprising people with your sharp memory and minty fresh breath.

Bad Habits that Slow Memory and Decrease Productivity

Smoking and Drinking

Smoking and excessive drinking can have negative impacts on memory. The impairment that is associated with using these substances is more than using just one of these. Basically, it is a double whammy.

Research has shown that excessively drinking more than 14 servings in one week plus smoking can cause numerous negative memory and health problems. This means that if you are a man and drink more than eight servings at one time plus you smoke you are doing a lot of damage to your body. For a female, it would be six servings.

Excessively drinking alcohol will damage prospective memory. A group of volunteers was asked to hand a scientist a book after giving a cue or calling a specific number at a certain time: volunteers who binge drank didn't remember to carry out as many actions as a volunteer who didn't drink at all. Similar patterns were also found with people who smoked. People who smoke every day won't carry out as many actions as people who haven't ever smoked.

Drinking to excess and smoking will impair memory if used separately, but when they are used together, it intensifies the effects. Smoking can worsen memories of people who drink alcohol excessively. People who smoke and drink will have more memory problems, won't be able to think fast or effectively, and will have problems solving puzzles. People who are addicted to cigarettes and alcohol will have more brain damage than people who don't. People who are addicted will have a thinning in the frontal cortex. This part of the brain controls memory.

Polydrug Users

Since most people will drink and smoke, the effects were tested to see how what negative effects it had on prospective memory. Four groups of volunteers were tested: a control group that didn't smoke or drink, people who smoke and drank to excess, people who smoke but didn't drink that often, and people who drank to excess but didn't smoke. These volunteers were tested to see if they could remember to do six actions. In three of these the volunteers were asked to do a specific task at a certain time like "In six minutes, you need to pick up the blue pen." The other three the volunteers were asked to do a specific action when given a certain cue like "When you get to a question about cheese, please hand the book to me." They were asked to do these while working on puzzles.

The final analysis showed the people who drank to excess and smoked had more impairment than the other groups. This means that things happen when using these substances that will impact the memory negatively.

This study was the first to show how these substances affect prospective remembering. This is important since it shows prospective memory can be compromised when a person smokes and drinks excessively.

We hope these findings will improve people's understanding of how dangerous smoking and drinking is beyond the normal public warnings about health.

Exercise

There are many great reasons to be active physically. The main ones are reducing the chances of developing diabetes, stroke, and heart disease. You might want to look better, prevent depression, lower your blood pressure, or lose weight. You might be experiencing brain fog that comes as we age. The good news is that exercising can change the way the brain protects its thinking and memory skills.

Researchers have found that doing aerobic exercises regularly, the ones that make you sweat and gets your heart pumping; will give a boost to the hippocampus. This part of the brain helps with learning and verbal memory. Muscle toning, balance, and resistance training won't give you the same results.

This is needed since scientists say one person is diagnosed with dementia every four seconds somewhere in the world. They have estimated that by 2050 there will be more than 115 million people in the world with dementia.

Exercise can help thinking and memory by both indirect and direct ways. The benefits come from the brain's ability to stimulate a chemical that affects how healthy our brain cells are, grow new blood vessels, and even helps new brain cells to survive. The brain can also reduce inflammation and insulin resistance.

Exercising can also improve sleep and mood, along with reducing anxiety and stress. Any problems in any of these areas can cause cognitive impairment.

Many studies have shown that the medial temporal cortex and the prefrontal cortex that controls memory and thinking will be larger in people that exercise when compared to people who don't. If you regularly exercise for six months to a year, you will have more volume in certain regions of the brain.

So, what exactly do you need to do? Begin exercising. There aren't any specific exercises that are better than others. Most of the research looked at walkers. Basically, any form of aerobic exercise that will get your heart pumping will give you the same results.

How long and how often do you need to exercise? Most of the volunteers were asked to walk briskly for one hour two times each week. That totals to 120 minutes of moderate intensity exercise every week. Some recommend that 30 minutes of moderate physical activity for five days each week or around 150 minutes would be best. If that seems to be too hard, begin with ten minutes every day and increase until you get to 30 minutes.

If you don't like walking, think about dancing, squash, tennis, climbing stairs, or swimming. Remember that chores around the house can count, too. Raking leaves, mopping, sweeping, or whatever gets your heart rate up and makes you sweat.

If you don't think you can do this by yourself, try some of these:

- Hire a personal trainer if you are financially able.
- Keep track of your progress to motivate you to get to your goal.
- Find a work out friend or class that holds you accountable.

It doesn't matter what motivates you, just choose an exercise and commit to creating a habit just like remembering to take your medication. As the old saying goes exercise is medicine, and this should be at the top of anybody's list as their number one reason to work out.

Sleep

When talking about the effects on memory, sleep can be a Goldilocks problem meaning that both too little and too much are not good. Try to find the "just right."

Getting a normal amount of sleep around seven hours a night might help maintain memory later on in life. Sleep therapy needs to be looked at to help prevent mental impairment.

A group of volunteers took part in a Nurse's Health Study and were asked to keep track of their sleep habits in 1986 and 2000. These people were interviewed about their thinking skills and memory three times within a six-year period. Researchers say that people who only slept five or fewer hours each night or slept longer than nine hours had worse performance as compared to people who got around seven or eight hours of sleep. Researchers said that people who either overslept or underslept were two years older mentally than people who got around seven or eight hours each night.

Beyond Memory

One study could actually prove that getting too much or little sleep causes thinking or memory problems. This is in line with other studies showing the harmful effects of poor sleep habits. Some research has shown that poor sleep can lead to depression, type 2 diabetes, stroke, and heart disease.

How does sleep affect memory? People that are sleep deprived could have narrowed blood vessels, diabetes, and high blood pressure. Any of these could decrease blood flow in the brain. The cells of the brain need plenty of sugar and oxygen so when there is a problem with blood flow it will affect the brain's ability to function the right way.

Poor sleep can affect the brain in other ways. When the brain is sleep deprived, it can cause deposits of beta-amyloid to build up. Beta-amyloid is a protein that can cause a decline in thinking and memory and increases the risk of developing dementia.

What if you get too much sleep? If you get more than ten hours of sleep each night, often have poor sleep quality. The most important numbers might not be how much sleep but the quality of sleep you are getting.

Another possibility is the two way street between memory and sleep: the quality of sleep can affect thinking and memory along with the changes in the brain that causes thinking, and memory problems could disrupt sleep.

Better Sleep

Here are some tips to help you get a better quality of sleep:

- Create a relaxing bedtime routine along with a specific time: listen to calming music or take a warm bubble bath.

- Use the bed for lovemaking or sleeping. Don't watch television or read in bed.

- Make sure your bedroom is quiet and dark and your bed is comfy. You could use earplugs or a sleep mask if you need to.

- If you aren't asleep in 20 minutes, get out of bed and go to a different room. Find something that relaxes you. Never get turn on your tablet, computer, or television. Once you begin to feel sleepy, go back to bed. Never delay your wake-up time to try and make up any sleep that was lost.

- Stay away from alcohol after dinner. Many people think it is a sedative, but it can affect your quality sleep.

- Exercise. Try to get around 30 minutes of moderate exercise each day. Try to do this early in the day. Try doing some yoga or stretches to help relax your mind and muscles close to bedtime.

- To keep from having to use the bathroom a lot during the night, avoid any fluids after dinner.

- When you can do any demanding or stressful tasks early in your day and less demanding activities later. This can help you wind down after a hard day.

- Limit your caffeine intake and don't drink any after 2 pm.

- Never go to bed hungry and never eat a large meal just before going to bed. If you need a snack, make sure it is light and bland.

Try to practice relaxed breathing. Use slow breaths when exhaling.

Conclusion

Thanks for making it through to the end of *Memory and Accelerated Learning*. Let's hope it was informative and able to provide you with all of the tools you need to achieve your goals whatever they may be.

Remember learning and memory can be improved and increased through simple action steps. It's not static. It's growing and changing your entire life. Increased learning ability will help you to learn more things with ease and less frustration. When coupled with improved memory, you will be amazed at the things you will be able to achieve. Think about learning a new language. How easy would it be with better memory? You would be less likely to give up when things get hard.

First things first, though, you have to make sure that you maintain a single focus. Multi-tasking is a myth that people think they have mastered. Your mind is only able to focus on a single task at a time, and jumping around from task to task isn't getting anything done faster. All you will end up feeling is frustrated. Figure out the one thing that you need to focus on, and work on it until it is finished.

When it comes to memory, don't forget that the more senses you involve in remembering something, the easier it will be to remember it when the time comes. Create a mental picture that you would never be able to forget. Make it as crazy as you possibly can.

Don't think that imagination is something that only children can use. Imagination has always been, and will always be, a very powerful skill in anything and everything that you do. It helps you remember and learn things. That's why teachers will use pictures alongside information to help people remember what they are learning. Images are powerful tools for the human mind, and so often, people forget their power.

Besides learning how to use a mental image and your imagination, you can also create mind maps. These are not only helpful for learning, but they are also fun to make. The simple rote method of learning has failed people for far too long. Mind mapping is the new way to remember and learn things, so use it and reap its amazing benefits.

Remember that increasing your reading speed is another viable option is accelerating your learning. You will not only be able to learn more in a shorter amount of time, but you will also retain more information. Now, keep in mind, you don't have to use speed reading all the time, and there are times when you shouldn't speed read. If you are reading for fun, then there is really no need for speed reading. Also, if it's an important work document that you have to thoroughly go over and present something on it, then it is best to not speed read either. The main thing is to make sure that you use these skills you have learned at the right time.

When it comes down to it, though, if you can't maintain your memories, what good are they? Once you have grasped the ability to increase your learning and improve your memory, the time has come to make sure you don't forget those things. This is probably the most overlooked part of the learning process. People think once they have learned something that it will always be there when they need. While in some cases this may be true, it's not always true for everybody.

If you don't access and use the information you have learned from time to time, it will leave you. You've heard the saying, if you don't use it, you'll lose it. Well, that's how memories work. If you don't have to use a memory, then just look back over it from time to time. When you learn a new language, you don't just read the words in a book. You speak them out loud. While you may not be around another person that speaks that language, you can still speak it just for fun. This will make sure that you remember the language when the time comes for you to use it.

Lastly, you have to make sure that you give up the habit of procrastination. Sure, it's super easy to do. Why else would so many people cause themselves distress if it wasn't? Everybody does, but very few try to stop it. Some allow it to affect their lives so much that it affects their jobs and relationships. Nobody wants to hear the words, "You're fired," but that's exactly where severe procrastination can lead you. Do whatever it is that you have to do to make sure that you get rid of procrastination and turn it into productivity. Remember, this doesn't have to mean that you are mean to yourself and force yourself to work endlessly. This can be fun where you schedule yourself some procrastination breaks.

The important thing in all of this is to go easy on yourself. Everything that you have learned can improve your life, but it will take time and effort on your part. Take it slow, and remember that you can achieve a better memory and learning ability. It will happen. Kicking those other bad habits will help as well. While that may be easier said than done, it's important to your mind. As you have learned, excessive smoking and drinking don't serve you in any way. Lack of sleep and exercise also hurts your mind, both of which can be easily remedied.

Baby steps are what will get you where you need to be. Leaps and bounds will leave you frustrated, and you will probably give up. Nothing happens overnight, so make sure that you go at your own speed.

Get started using these techniques that you have learned. You will be amazed at what you can accomplish in life. Before you know it, you will have learned a new language, another habit, a musical instrument, whatever your heart desires.

Finally, if you found this useful in any way, a review on Amazon is always appreciated!

www.ingramcontent.com/pod-product-compliance
Lightning Source LLC
Chambersburg PA
CBHW071924290426
44110CB00013B/1461